THE
NEXT
AMERICAN
CITY

THE
NEXT
AMERICAN
CITY

The Big Promise
of Our Midsize Metros

MICK CORNETT

with JAYSON WHITE

G. P. PUTNAM'S SONS
New York

G. P. PUTNAM'S SONS
Publishers Since 1838
An imprint of Penguin Random House LLC
375 Hudson Street
New York, New York 10014

LIBRARY OF CONGRESS CATALOGING-IN-PUBLICATION DATA

Names: Cornett, Mick, author. | White, Jayson, author.
Title: The next American city: the big promise of our midsize metros / Mick Cornett with Jayson White.
Description: New York: G. P. Putnam's Sons, 2018. | Identifiers: LCCN 2018022150 | ISBN 9780399575099 (hardback) | ISBN 9780399575105 (epub)
Subjects: LCSH: City planning—United States. | Cities and towns—Growth. | Sociology, Urban—United States. | BISAC: SOCIAL SCIENCE / Sociology / Urban. | POLITICAL SCIENCE / Public Policy / City Planning & Urban Development. | HISTORY / United States / General.
Classification: LCC HT167 .C676 2018 | DDC 307.1/2160973—dc23
LC record available at https://lccn.loc.gov/2018022150
p.   cm.

Printed in the United States of America
10 9 8 7 6 5 4 3 2 1

Book design by Nancy Resnick
Set in Fairfield Medium

To Carroll and Nona Cornett,
who taught their youngest child
to work hard, dream big, and give back

Contents

Foreword by Richard Florida   ix

Preface: The Next American City: Three Transformations, Under Way   xv

Introduction: Leading from the Middle   1
    The Wrath of Grapes: America's Next Great Move to the Middle   14

CHAPTER ONE: Building a City, Beyond Boom and Bust   27
    New Orleans: The Rhythm and Ritual of City Strength   36

CHAPTER TWO: The Best Thing That Never Happened   43
    Seattle: WPPSS! How the Emerald City's Missteps Created Sustainability   59

CHAPTER THREE: Government We Want to Pay For   67
    Albuquerque: A Better Way to Fight Poverty and Homelessness   87

CHAPTER FOUR: From Mow to Row   93
    Des Moines: Embracing History for a Riverfront Renaissance   107

CHAPTER FIVE: Making the Big Leagues   115
    Sacramento: Can Kevin Save the Kings?   131

CHAPTER SIX: Where Leaders Come From   141
    Buffalo: A Perfect Advocate for an Imperfect Place   151

CHAPTER SEVEN: Putting the City on a Diet   157

    Louisville: Building a Culture of Compassion   176

CHAPTER EIGHT: Building for the Future   181

    Chattanooga: Investing in People—Every City's Greatest Asset   197

CHAPTER NINE: Punching Above Our Weight   207

    Charleston: We Knew You'd Come If You Could   220

Conclusion: The Path to Public Service   225

Acknowledgments   251

Foreword

A funny thing happened in the early years of the millennium. A rising global economy, alongside powerful new technologies that connected corners of the globe in an instant, would make it possible for us to live and work virtually anywhere we wanted. It seemed all but certain that the forces that were connecting our world would flatten it, too, and continue to push people apart.

Well, those forces did the opposite. They drove us closer together, not farther apart. They brought us back to cities and to urban life.

The twentieth century was the century of suburbanization: the flight from cities of people and industry, commerce and jobs as far from downtowns as our cars and highways could take us. The American Dream was then a vision of a big house and a car followed by a bigger house, two cars, and more. A big plot of land you could call your own. It was life on America's next great frontier, what the urban historian Kenneth Jackson called the "crabgrass frontier." As a young boy growing up in New Jersey, I watched my hometown of Newark decline. I saw the city erupt into riots; I saw the factory where my father worked shutter; I saw the newspaper where my mom worked, *The Star-Ledger*, ringed with barbed-wire fences. Between 1950 and 1980, Boston lost almost 30 percent of its population. After the "Boeing Bust," Seattle's unemployment reached as high as 25 percent. In 1975, New York City—while still arguably the world's most powerful global center of business and corporate finance—nearly declared bankruptcy. One of my professors at Rutgers wrote an article provocatively titled "The City as Sandbox," which argued that America's cities had become hollowed-out shells, having lost their core economic functions to the suburbs.

But now, shockingly, the twenty-first century has been deemed the "century of the city." Young people, professionals, and a growing predominance of scientists, techies, knowledge workers, and artists, designers, and media types—a group I named the "creative class"—have streamed back to cities in ways no one anticipated. Major companies are heading back to cities in droves. And even start-up companies are abandoning their tech-driven "nerdistans" in suburban office parks for the vibrancy and hubbub of urban centers.

So far, it is fairly clear that large cities and metropolitan areas have benefited disproportionately from this urban shift. The first two decades of this urban revival have been marked by "winner-take-all urbanism" wherein a relatively small number of superstar cities like New York and London and knowledge centers like San Francisco, Boston, and Seattle have attracted the largest concentrations of talent, ideas, investment, and economic activity.

However, the reality is that the new urban knowledge economy is not determined by size alone. In fact, population size and population growth are poor predictors of innovation and economic growth. And as our largest urban centers become increasingly expensive, unaffordable, and divided, they price out and drive away the very diversity that powered their innovativeness and growth to begin with. As the late great urbanist Jane Jacobs once told me, "When a place gets boring, even the rich people leave."

It's a big mistake to write off small places. College towns in particular have boomed, as have a host of smaller and midsize cities, even rural areas. Size may be an advantage but it is not the sole determinant of success. Smaller places that cultivate innovation and creativity, have abundant natural or urban amenities, and connect to larger centers in the United States and the world are thriving.

The reality of our time is that the world is spiky—not flat. While technology may have flattened *access* to ideas and information, the reality of our time is that access to *opportunity* has become increasingly spiky in this urban century. And this spikiness occurs across all scales. Some large places—the ones we all know and talk about—are doing fine, but others are struggling. And the same goes for small and medium-size cities and rural areas. Some thrive, others coast along, and many others decline.

After years of study, I've concluded that the key thing that distinguishes the thriving places of any and all sizes is surprisingly simple. Successful places are intentional. They undertake efforts to leverage and build upon their own unique assets. They mobilize their anchor institutions, their own civic organizations, and their people. They build true public-private partnerships. And, large or small, they create a genuine quality of place that all can see and feel.

As I travel to places like Milwaukee and Des Moines and Boise and Oklahoma City, my former hometown of Pittsburgh, my wife's hometown of Detroit, and countless others across America,

I see the incredible progress many so-called flyover places have made. And now I watch as even smaller communities—like Bentonville or El Dorado, Arkansas (the latter chronicled in these very pages)—do much the same to leverage their own knowledge assets or lakefronts and hillsides or arts communities to create their own renaissance. It can be done. It is being done. It does take money. And smart policy. And great local leaders. But above all, it takes intentional leadership to mobilize the energy of the community to do it.

In the decade or so since writing *The Rise of the Creative Class*, I watched Mick Cornett mobilize his community in just that way during his four terms as mayor of Oklahoma City. If you've heard of him at all, it's likely from the time he famously energized his community by putting the entire town on a diet to encourage fitness and vitality—long before "wellness" became a watchword of the new urbanism. His accomplishments go far beyond that single story, however. Cornett was the longest serving in a long line of fiscally conservative Oklahoma City mayors that have understood the importance of a city investing in itself in this new urban, talent-driven age. While maintaining his focus on balanced budgets and sound economic policy, this Republican leader understood when, and how, local taxes could effectively and uniquely fund local infrastructure and improve the quality of place and quality for his community.

You see, local leadership really does defy party. As I like to say, when I meet a national politician, it is immediately clear which side of the political divide they're on. But when I travel to cities across the United States, I am amazed I can never tell who is a Democrat and who is a Republican. Is it any wonder that at a time when less than a fifth of Americans have any trust and confidence in our federal government, that as many as three-quarters of us still have trust and confidence in our local governments? That's because we get to pick where we live—we "vote with our feet," to use that famous phrase—to pick the kind of place that best suits us and our families. We get to choose our local leadership, and we are close to that local leadership too. Localism, not nationalism, is the essence of the American experiment.

The incredible efforts to revitalize America's great, small, and medium-size places are revealed in this book, *The Next American City*. It shows the enormous potential of smaller cities—and how that potential can be, and is being, unlocked. America is different from other nations precisely because it is not dominated by a single city. New York, for example, produces just 10 percent of America's economic output, while Toronto produces 20 percent of Canada's, London more than a third of the UK's, and Seoul more than half of South Korea's.

One of the great sources of strength and diversity in America is its constellation of great communities, large and small, urban and rural, with unique strengths and capabilities. What truly distinguishes America and really makes it great is the incredible diversity of its more than 350 metro areas and thousands of communities of various sizes and shapes. These are the true laboratories of democracy, where new and transformative ideas, strategies, and visions of the future bubble up.

Above all, this book offers a vision of America made up of great places full of creative people producing big ideas, building their own communities, and creating new purpose. That, in a nutshell, is the new American Dream—and in these pages you will find a rallying call for urban optimism at a time when it is so badly needed.

Richard Florida

Preface
The Next American City:
Three Transformations, Under Way

A new frontier is opening in America. As our nation's population grows, and our cities swell with ideas, energy, and creativity, the world is changing before our eyes. Over the past twenty years, I was fortunate to serve my city, travel the world, and witness three incredible transformations under way.

The first has been the rebirth of my own hometown. What was once a hopeless place on the brink of collapse has become a vibrant, growing, diverse American city. For generations, we rode the waves of boom and bust, and our fortunes rose and fell with the price of a barrel of oil. After suffering a devastating attack on our nation and way of life in 1995, Oklahomans did as Americans often do. We joined hands and dared the world to tear us apart.

The reinvention of Oklahoma City has been nothing short of a miracle. We rebuilt every school in the inner city. We revived "the downtown ditch the grown-ups called the river." We redesigned our city and downtown around people rather than the automobile—constructing enough sidewalks and trails to walk to Dallas if we laid them in a straight line. We changed in a matter of years from a wounded city with no national brand to a truly "big-league city." The tide has turned in OKC. And we are proud of it.

The second transformation surprised me even more. As momentum built in my hometown, I crisscrossed the country and traveled the globe to spread word of the city's renaissance. On those trips I thought I might be teaching others—but I learned much more than I could ever have hoped to share.

What I learned was this: Smaller cities across the country and around the world are changing at a breakneck pace. Technology and talent are flourishing. Next-generation infrastructure is being built. People are flocking—by the hundreds of thousands—from our coastal capitals to the nation's new growing home in the heartland. And the one hundred or so rising metros are adding immeasurably to the diversity of our country's culture, richness of opportunities, and widened access to the American Dream. It may be hard to see from the Silicon Valley, a Wall Street boardroom, or an ivory tower, but I assure you the reinvention of Middle America is real.

The third transformation has been my own. My career began as a sportscaster for a local TV station in a happy and hopeful but declining city that had no major-league team and was failing to share its story with the outside world. I loved my hometown, but as I got older, I started to understand that most of the kids I attended high school and college with were leaving Oklahoma behind. On-air, my persona evolved into a lighthearted, comedic style, but behind the scenes I burned out and cut a path to public service. I wanted my life to mean something. And I knew my city was capable of so much more. Taking that leap taught me a lot. About hard work, leadership, and what it takes to make a difference.

I learned these lessons leading a city that once bled graduates, investment, and opportunity to bigger cities and faraway places. We have become a magnet for talent, companies, and big ideas once again. And we did it primarily by dreaming big, working hard, and choosing to invest in ourselves.

In this, Oklahoma City is far from alone. We are, I believe, in the early days of a new golden age for the American city, where a hundred cities, maybe even more, will find their way to a future brighter than they could have ever imagined. How it works, who's in charge, and where it is happening fastest may surprise you just as much as it has surprised me.

Mick Cornett
Oklahoma City, Oklahoma

Introduction: Leading from the Middle

By the winter of 2008, I knew the drill. With four years as mayor of Oklahoma City and twenty years as a sportscaster and news anchor under my belt, I had done twenty thousand newscasts and thousands of interviews. I'd interviewed hundreds of people myself—and sometimes those people were not in a very good mood. As mayor, I'd won heated campaign debates, faced angry citizens in city council meetings, testified in the United States Congress, and talked policy with the president of the United States.

But sitting backstage that day, I was as nervous as I had ever been. I was about to go on *Ellen.*

Interestingly enough, I wasn't the only one making my first appearance with Ellen that day. Ellen's "headline" guest was a fresh-faced eighteen-year-old country singer I had never even heard of before. But her stories about breaking up with one of the Jonas Brothers mesmerized the crowd. It was probably going to be a breakthrough day for Taylor Swift. I was crossing my fingers that it would be for me, too.

Besides the fact that I was just some mayor of a small city in the middle of nowhere, I faced a deeper challenge: the subject I'd been invited to talk about. I was there to talk about being fat.

Or I guess more accurately, about getting real and losing some weight. And not just my personal weight-loss journey, either. Other politicians had done that much before.

I was there to talk about an oddball idea I'd had just a couple months earlier. Without any authority, or reason to know for sure it would work, I'd done something that was borderline nuts. I'd gone to our city's zoo, stood in front of the elephants, and put my entire city on a diet.

Being a relatively new mayor, I had reasons to be risk-averse. This was—no doubt about it—risky. A calculated choice, but risky nonetheless. A lighthearted take on a serious subject. The country was beginning to focus on obesity. I figured we could either be an example of the problem or an example of a city that was not afraid to do tough things.

My feeling was that the first step toward actually dealing with obesity was to start a conversation about it. But as I sat backstage in my oversize dressing room waiting for my chance to talk to a few million people all at once, I started second-guessing myself.

It was pretty lonely back there. This dressing room had my name on the door and was large enough for an entourage of ten people. I guess most guests on *Ellen* bring a couple of limos full of support staff. I was all by myself. Just me, my backpack, and my doubts—the last of which were growing by the minute. If I'd wanted to distract myself, the table and the refrigerator were fully stocked with snacks. But that was no help at all. Like the rest of my city, I was on a diet.

The irony continued. This should have been one of the most exciting times of my life—a TV journalist turned mayor of my hometown! About to go on *Ellen*! I had been preparing for this for my whole life.

Ellen DeGeneres was already a red-carpet, A-list celebrity at the top of her game. This interview would be in front of a Los Angeles studio audience (not to mention millions of viewers at home) who were all expecting something good. I had arrived with material I thought would be funny. But as her producers rehearsed with me how the interview would go, I realized I didn't need to be funny. I was the straight man, and she was the comedienne. I just kept telling myself, *"Relax."*

For all that pressure, I couldn't lose focus. Somehow, I needed to break through the noise and turn this five-minute interview into some real positive attention for my city.

I reminded myself that I was a veteran of television. I had thousands of hours of TV news and sports under my belt. Most of them had gone exceptionally well. Sure, every once in a while, there would be a disaster. Twenty-five years earlier, my first TV boss once tried to console me after my sportscast completely fell apart live on the air.

"You know, when you are in a car wreck, sometimes you don't get to get up and walk away," he reminded me. "That's the good thing about television," he continued. "No matter how bad it is, you can always get up and walk away. So it can't be that bad."

There was a knock on the dressing room door. It was time. A stagehand was ready to walk me toward the stage. He seemed surprised that I was all alone in that big room. I asked if I could leave my backpack and get it on my way out. He thought that was funny.

As I stood behind the curtain waiting to be introduced, Ellen joked about what the city's weight-loss plan might actually be.

"I hope he isn't just asking them to move away!" she cracked.

That was funny. I could tell by the crowd's laughter, and I laughed myself as I stood backstage. But what really hit me in the interview was that she and her audience were not laughing *at us*. They were laughing *with us*.

Then Ellen brought me onstage.

"When a survey ranked Oklahoma City as one of the fattest cities in the nation, our next guest sprang into action, asking the residents to lose one million pounds. Please welcome the mayor of Oklahoma City, Mick Cornett."

The Wrong Lists at the Wrong Time

The plan worked. Something about this initiative put our city on the national stage for a moment. And for the first time in a long time, if we played this thing right, it could be the kind of attention we wanted.

I'm not sure I would have seen it then, either, but a lot of cities across Middle America were on the cusp of big ideas and bigger changes. The willingness to take a risk and invest in our future was a bigger trend than I could have ever seen on my own.

But those bigger changes in smaller cities were already afoot. Around the time I was elected in 2004, Oklahoma City was starting to emerge as a community worth noticing. The city was just on the verge of coming out of the economic slumber and boom-and-bust cycle that had driven many young adults and highly productive professionals of my own generation—and the companies they worked for—to leave town for bigger and brighter places.

How did I know we were turning the corner? We were starting to show up on "the lists."

The lists? Take a look at the bottom of any webpage, and you'll probably see a link to one of those top-ten lists and city rankings the mainstream media and clickbait bloggers love to put out every week.

Bloggers love to rank cities. And mayors, and evidently readers, too, like to see where we stack up against the competition.

Up to that time Oklahoma City had so rarely made any positive list that when I first noticed us appearing anywhere them, it was kinda cool!

> #4 Best City to Get a Job!
> #2 Best City to Start a Business!
> #7 Coolest Downtown!
> #5 Best-Tasting Drinking Water!

At the time we weren't number one on any of these lists, but just to appear on them was great PR for the city. We joked at city hall that we were finally "somebody"!

And then came the one list on which no mayor wanted to see their city. The list of the Fattest Cities in America.

There we were, right near the top. OMG.

Now, I'd like to point out that we were on that list with a lot of really cool places! Dallas, Houston, Atlanta, New Orleans, Miami. All places I'd love to take a vacation. These weren't cities that you'd typically be afraid to be associated with.

But still . . . I didn't like being on *that* list. What I decided to do about it defied the laws of PR in a way and brought national attention to one of these forgotten Middle American cities. Not for showing up in the middle of the pack on some arbitrary ranking, but for our willingness to face our flaws *and then do something about it.*

That day on *Ellen,* Oklahoma City was worth talking about. And since then even more cities and metros, as small as ten thousand and as big as one million, that most Americans call home are doing the same. Facing their weaknesses, deciding to see them as opportunities, and taking action. This may just be one of the most exciting trends in America in generations.

From Good to Great? Try "Worst to First"

It took several years of work before my hometown started showing up on "the lists." But in the twenty years since the Oklahoma City bombing, our city has gone through a lot of change. Almost all of that change has been for the better. Most of it has been truly remarkable.

I like to say it this way: Our community of change-makers has taken our economy, our downtown, our city, our standards, and our view of the future "from worst to first."

In just a few short years, the people of Oklahoma City built a beautiful new downtown baseball park, saving our AAA baseball team. We also built a new central library; rebuilt our performing arts center, convention center, and fairground facilities. We built the Bricktown entertainment district along a canal (that we also built) next to what for decades had been a dry patch of grass that adults had a habit of calling "the river."

We rebuilt every school in the OKC school district, with tremendous support from our suburban communities to focus on the inner-city schools in greatest need of investment.

And there's more. A lot more, really, but in the end we invested over $5 billion (and what feels like as many hours) in public and private money, creating what *National Geographic* called the "Pride of the Plains" on its 2015 list of the best vacation destinations in the world. Trust me—growing up in Oklahoma City, we thought of ourselves more as a truck stop than an international vacation destination.

From the depths of our financial struggles of the early 1990s and the devastating attack on the Alfred P. Murrah Federal Building, Oklahoma City has risen from very likely the worst economy in the country to one of the strongest, most resilient, diverse—and proud—places there is. But this transformation is a lot more common than you'd think: and maybe even a little bit easier than it looks.

The Big Idea:
Small Places, Punching Above Our Weight

Some version of the "turnaround" story is at the heart of the history of most of the great cosmopolitan capitals and global gateway cities in our nation today. Cities like Boston were rocked, not necessarily for the first time in their history, by globalization in the middle of the twentieth century. Between 1950 and 1980, populations shifted south and west and textile and manufacturing jobs moved overseas. Boston shrank by nearly 30 percent in population. As this trend grew nationwide, many city leaders and national pundits wondered aloud if the age of urbanism was over.

Not only has Boston turned around its population growth—something any mayor will tell you is absolutely essential for a city's future—they have found their footing for the next century in a diverse economy, inventive higher education, incredible institutions, and an increasingly global reach.

In this transformation, Boston is not alone—nor will it be the last city to find its competitive advantage in the needs of growing companies and families in a quickly changing world. In truth, this pattern has played out in its own way in almost all of the great cities Americans treasure.

For example, in Seattle in the early 1970s times were much darker than they are now. Boeing, following years of growth in a dramatically expanding economy, suffered major setbacks and laid off more than forty thousand workers in a year's time. Unemployment in the Emerald City reached as high as 25 percent. Business leaders were seriously worried the city would clear out completely. And long before there was such a thing as an Internet millionaire or anything called Amazon.com, there was a billboard on the road to the airport that read WILL THE LAST PERSON LEAVING SEATTLE—TURN OUT THE LIGHTS.

We know the rest of the story there. Seattle has found its way. And the same basic narrative has played out in cities like Charlotte, Portland (Oregon), Denver, Atlanta, Nashville, and my own city.

When times are tough, good places with great people dig deep and find a way to blaze a trail to the future. And it is this sort of adventure that hundreds of mayors and cities find themselves in the beginning stages of today.

Big Enough for Scale, Small Enough for Change

The turnaround story for cities is by no means a special territory of smaller or midsize cities, to be sure. Who can forget the heroic efforts of Mayor Rudolph Giuliani in New York or Mayor Ed Rendell in Philadelphia in the 1990s? At a time in our nation's history when cities were far from the hubs of innovation and opportunity we see them as today, leaders like these truly achieved the impossible.

But in part because the reality is that most Americans live in our country's smaller and midsize cities, and in part because of some new, exciting ideas growing in these places, a true revolution is coming that will shape the way we think about the fabric of our nation for decades to come.

For the sake of this book, I'd like for you to think of Middle America not so much as the Midwest, or "flyover" landlocked places, but as the cities wherever they sit where most of our citizens and families live, work, and play.

Those smaller markets and cities that the vast majority of Americans call home. Now, a range between ten thousand and a million residents might seem quite wide, but just ask anyone from Indianapolis or Columbus (both about eight hundred and fifty thousand residents) whether they feel more at home in Manhattan, New York, or Manhattan, Kansas.

The city turnarounds and stories of new growth you'll read in these pages are not just more common than you'd think. They are increasingly replicable, and build on assets that hundreds, maybe thousands of cities have. The tools and allies are more practiced and available than ever. And what really drives this change is our communities' openness, optimism, resilience, and diversity. These exceptional traits of our country and our economy are the only tools you'll ever really need.

The truth is that hundreds of mayors and other leaders are sparking the changes at the individual level that are getting everybody "pulling on the same rope" to make the impossible happen. Individual people, with simple ideas, can move the dial and inspire hundreds, even thousands, to focus their work. Or, like me, to change their cities in positive ways.

The track record is long as well. Each of the great Middle

American cities we all think of today have suffered great losses and come to the edge of disaster—or in a few cases way over it. In those times of trial, we find our footing and create new pathways to progress.

Partly because of the inspiration these stories provide—and partly because of some important new force that makes them simultaneously more possible and more powerful—these kinds of lasting turnarounds are on the horizon in many cities across the country, with big implications for the deepest challenges our country faces.

From my view, not from the top of a skyscraper along the nation's coastline, but from a city with more than a hundred thousand new residents with the energy and insight to match, I see a great future for this country and for the millions of Americans who call fast-growing cities like mine home.

Western cities like Tacoma, Tulsa, Salt Lake City, Fort Collins, and Boise are finding their footing in the global economy. Strong Midwest tech scenes are sprouting up in Fargo, Madison, Grand Rapids, and Bloomington. Across the Southwest, Las Vegas, Tucson, Albuquerque, and Santa Fe are growing in diversity, creativity, and economic strength. And across the South, Fayetteville, Memphis, Jackson, and Birmingham offer an incredible quality of life, at a price that an aspiring middle class will flock to for a generation.

In a word, cities that once might have remained on the sidelines, hoping to benefit from the offshoots of opportunities born in New York, Los Angeles, or Chicago, now have the ability to take center stage. It is entirely possible to create a truly innovative company with a truly global reach that attracts (or builds) world-class talent in a place far away from the country's cultural and economic "capitals."

In fact, there is an advantage in working away from the

spotlight. In these emerging mid-market dynamos like Chattanooga, Tennessee, or Provo, Utah, or Boise, Idaho, you find yourself in a place where your ideas can truly take flight, yet have the time to live and the space you need for your biggest ideas to come together.

Another way of putting it is that these new, powerful mid-market cities are places that are plenty big for ambitious ideas to scale, yet small enough to embrace change, and act fast, when the time for our great ideas has come.

"The Middle" Is Where the Action Is

That was a pretty inspiring little speech, right? A nice new look at Middle America. Far beyond cities like mine in the center of the country, these new middles can inspire a lot of hope for a lot of people.

But are we really supposed to believe that the frontier for America's future is "the middle"? Not a very exciting place to be, right? Who wants to be in the middle of the pack? Who wants to be in between anything? The word itself is kind of anticlimactic. Middle school is a total horror. The middle child gets left out of everything. The middle finger? We won't get into that.

Well, I'm here to tell you that the middle is actually a great place to be. These new middles are where most of the country's growth and innovation are currently happening, and will likely continue to for years to come.

For four terms and fourteen years, I was the middle-aged mayor of a midsize city that sits in what many people consider the middle of nowhere. Along the way, though, I've watched our city go from a place many associated with disappointment and devastation to become a city on the cutting edge.

When I first took office, if you asked people what came to mind when they thought about Oklahoma City, the next word would be something bad. The Oklahoma City *bombing*. The Oklahoma City *tornado*. Not many people had much more in mind about Oklahoma than bad weather, a good musical, a great book, and a moment of tremendous national tragedy.

Now though, when I meet interesting people, they want to talk to me about Russell Westbrook's amazing MVP season and how far the Oklahoma City Thunder will advance this year. They ask about the new Devon tower, the largest skyscraper in all of the plains. Visitors to town want to stroll along the Bricktown Canal, ride the exciting class IV whitewater rapids at the USRowing National High Performance Center, attend the annual NCAA Women's College World Series, or check out the National Cowboy & Western Heritage Museum. They want to see local recording artists like Toby Keith, Parker Millsap, or Wayne Coyne's Flaming Lips, or visit the Oklahoma City Museum of Art. They might be one of the twenty-five-thousand-plus runners in town each year to participate in the Oklahoma City Memorial Marathon.

But it's not just Oklahoma City where the tide has turned . . .

The Four Hidden Middles of American Life

How our city changed for the better in the past decade or so is a great story, well worth reading, but the bigger trends that make these urban turnarounds possible are critical for everyone in our country, if not the world, to understand.

As I've traveled across the country this past decade and a half, visiting dozens of mayors and cities, I've started noticing something interesting. The most ambitious projects, the most innovative companies, the most exciting changes, and the most inspiring leaders are showing up in the "middles" more often than at the tops.

And these middles I'm talking about aren't just in the land-locked states that *The New York Times* loves to call "flyover country." There are at least four major middles of American life that are growing and changing in dramatic ways:

- The seeds of change are blooming in the middle of the country—**but also in hundreds of midsize cities that dot the coasts.**
- Our nation's **midsize companies are growing at an incredible clip**—in an age when teams of twenty can build a company that takes on the world.
- Our country's middle class is **moving from mega-metros to smaller, more livable and manageable places.** While these people are often out of the spotlight, they still form the backbone of our economy and the foundation of our future.
- And the **pragmatic, productive, visionary politics** in smaller cities like my own (and probably yours) is getting things done and raising standards for millions of public servants at the local level.

It is in these hidden middles of American life where we are growing fastest, embracing change, solving problems, and making markets work for the best outcomes for all.

This is a story I have had the opportunity to share in dozens, maybe hundreds, of cities in the past twenty years of my life, and I believe building on this momentum is among the most important ideas our nation should rally behind in the coming decades.

The Wrath of Grapes: America's Next Great Move to the Middle

The story of growth and innovation in these "new middles" of American life is always a fun idea to share as I travel the country and talk with people. But there is another idea I think can help explain the power of the turnaround story and our current move to the middle in our minds. Near the end of just about every speech I give, I ask the audience if they have read a book. But not just any book. *The book.*

All right, it's not the Bible, but the book that went a long way in defining Oklahoma's image for more than eighty years: John Steinbeck's Pulitzer Prize–winning *The Grapes of Wrath*.

It doesn't matter if I am speaking to retirees in Rochester or millennials in Minneapolis. Whether I am speaking in Paris, Texas, or Paris, France. It never fails to amaze me that just about every English-speaking person in the audience has at least heard the outlines of Steinbeck's story.

It wasn't always immediately clear why the mayor of Oklahoma City might be asking about *The Grapes of Wrath*. For most people, that book is a distant memory from high school homework. For those that do remember it a bit more clearly, a hard-wrought life on the American Great Plains, the Dust Bowl, the Great Depression, and a family on a long journey to California come to mind.

For those of us who grew up in Oklahoma, it was a little different.

Sometimes I joke that reading that book was just something our teachers did to ensure that our kids would feel bad enough about themselves.

As it turns out, lots of schools think the book contains some real lessons to learn. And now, with surging growth and innovation in cities across Middle America on my mind, I agree even more than ever.

Remembering *The Grapes of Wrath*

The Grapes of Wrath is the story of a poor Oklahoma family in the 1930s. They have lost everything: their farm, their money, and any hope they might have been hanging on to.

The nation was in the depths of an environmental catastrophe and the midst of an economic meltdown. After a generation of high-flying times and record-breaking stock market returns, the future suddenly seemed dim. Everyday people struggled, while faraway bankers and capitalists controlled vast and growing wealth. Automated work from powerful new machines threatened the country's core industries. And together these changes cut to the heart of the basic promises that millions of Americans had built their lives upon.

Any of that sound familiar to you?

In response, the Joad family did what Americans do. The only thing they could. They moved.

Ma and Pa Joad gathered up their belongings and their loved ones and headed west. At the end of Route 66 and a thousand-mile journey was California. The Promised Land. There, they were assured, they would find prosperity and work. And a chance for their kids to have a better future.

Unfortunately, what the Joads found waiting in California was a far cry from what they had expected. Work was scarce and wages thin. Children starved and thousands died. The "locals," who themselves had arrived only a generation before, even passed a law to keep the Okies out.

Steinbeck's grandest irony? The land was verdant and the laborers willing to work. The harvests were incredibly heavy, but the fruit of the land and all that labor died on the vine. These were the grapes of wrath.

And while Steinbeck's story ends in California, we cannot forget the impact this chapter in our history had on the places left behind. In my hometown and home state, and maybe yours, this massive move in a single direction reversed generations of hard-won progress in hundreds of American cities.

And it happened not all that long ago—at the time of this book's publication, it is only about eighty years gone. It would be foolish to think of these as forgotten times, or circumstances to which our country cannot return.

There are many morals to Steinbeck's story. The damage that can occur when politics turns into finger-pointing rather than problem-solving. The dangers that people in power can pose to new and unfamiliar neighbors. The impact of technology and the disruptive changes it brings. The tragedy that unfolds in places left behind.

One more lesson I think we can learn is this: Too much of a good thing in one place can cause more harm than good.

A Nation in Search of a Narrative

While the Joads' story tells a devastating chapter in our history, it also reflects a key to our country's greatness. Americans move. We dream. When things get tough where we are, we blaze a trail to a better future.

First, we moved across the ocean to pursue our freedoms and settle the New World. That same vision pushed Americans across the continent to fulfill the ideal of Manifest Destiny. In subsequent generations, first miners, then farmers, migrants, and aspiring movie stars headed west to California in search of the American Dream.

Moving hasn't always been a good thing, though. While our country's growth across the continent welcomed many millions from around the globe to build a new nation, the forced relocation of Native American people at our forefathers' hands has created incredible pain that leaders in the American West are still trying to understand and work through today.

My own father moved west from Oklahoma in the summer of 1941 in search of work and a better life. From the stories he told, the future he found was not much better than the past he'd left behind. Of a group of five friends that made the trip together, only he found work stocking shelves in a drugstore. Occasionally he snuck food out the back door to his hungry friends who weren't so lucky. Dad's story has always stayed with me, but it wasn't until relatively recently I started thinking about how powerful mass movements have been in our national narrative.

So, it is with some delight that I now pore through the Census Bureau's statistics, looking at migration in the United States. And it appears that the grandkids of those thousands of families are coming back.

In the years since the Great Recession, thousands more people moved *from* California *to* Oklahoma City than vice versa. It seems to be true year after year, and the new residents are more than welcome. Back in Oklahoma City, I call it *The Wrath of Grapes.*

This is not just an Oklahoma phenomenon. By my look at the numbers, our nation's midsize metros are growing about 20 percent faster than the nation's largest urban centers. And when it comes to domestic migration, the change has really been quite remarkable. A recent Brookings Institution study showed that between 2010 and 2016, New York lost on net 900,000 people to domestic migration, Los Angeles almost 375,000, and Chicago a little over 400,000. A look at census data over that same period shows that among the top-ten fastest growing metros in the country, not a single top-ten metro is in the mix. Even in those biggest metros, the areas growing the fastest are the cities and suburbs around them that look a lot more like my hometown than the towering blocks of midtown Manhattan.

Immigrants, too, are no longer finding it necessary to land in our largest cities. That same Brookings study shows just how big an impact the new generation of immigrants, through hard work and industriousness, are having far away from the few cities that used to be their most common landing points. And in these midsize cities, these new Americans are finding quality work, cheaper housing, reliable public transportation—and a fertile environment for starting a business and accruing the wealth and opportunity that America's name has come to mean around the world. Not only this, but smaller cities now offer a more accepting, open culture and diverse community than they ever have before.

A Rising Tide, Lifting an Entire Nation

Usually, by about the time I share two or three facts like these with a friend from business school or a reporter who lives in New York, I can feel them bristling a little. I mean, *obviously*

New York is the only city in the world that matters. *Clearly* San Francisco's dominance in technology and venture capital will continue forever. The whole world is urbanizing! Smaller cities are a thing of the past! The rate at which my rent is going up in Seattle proves it: Everybody wants to live here!

I like to respond in a couple ways. First, I'm not a demographer, and I'm certainly not a prophet. The surge in populations moving from the very largest metro areas could reverse as it has before.

But the second, bigger point is really a question of what we should *want* as a country. If we are lucky enough to be growing both our population and our economy, and lucky enough to be attracting talented people from around the world to our shores, where should we want people to live? What kind of cities, and in how many places, should we be trying to build as a country?

For now, it appears there is a surge in interest, across generations, incomes, and walks of life, to build businesses, make homes, plan careers, and invest in communities across a broad range of places. This diversity will, I believe, make us stronger, and we should be fighting like mad to build on this momentum.

So the question to answer is: *Why?* Why are people in such significant numbers moving to smaller markets or to communities and suburbs around the biggest metros?

If you're on board with the idea that we can build a better America by building a broad array of cities—a constellation of great places dotting the map from coast to coast—then what ideas are working? What insights are truly helping those places build a brighter future?

Better housing prices, lighter traffic, and the proliferation of top-tier restaurants are all part of the story. But the more I learn and listen to people talk, the more convinced I become that the true answer is deeply connected to our story as a nation.

The American ideals of hope and entrepreneurship are the deeper driving factors. The same spirit of hope that brought the Pilgrims across the Atlantic to build a community around their beliefs and way of life. The same spirit of entrepreneurship that drew hundreds of thousands west to California is now drawing people to get in on the ground floor of the next great chapter of America's history: building the next American city.

This is not a zero-sum contest between the biggest places in the country and the rest of America. Instead, I am trying to tell a new and—I hope—inspiring tale of the dozens of places that are building quickly, actively, and creatively for the future. A few things hold these stories and their leaders together. We learn from our mistakes. We build our own brands. We grow our own leaders when we can—and invite newcomers with open arms when they arrive. At heart, we are working with what we have, to build the places where we want to live.

Case Studies: A Trip Through Flyover Country

So, if we start to understand why the middles of American life are growing so quickly, perhaps the next question becomes: *How?* How are cities around the country doing this? As mayor of Oklahoma City, I had the privilege not only to see my own hometown reinvent itself in creative and instructive ways but to visit numerous American cities that are doing the same in their own unique ways. Across the coming chapters, I'd like to take you on a tour of just a handful of these places.

In our first chapter, **"Building a City, Beyond Boom and Bust,"** together we will see that our futures are up to us, and great places draw from deep wells of strength. After long cycles of boom and bust, or after major tragedies hit cities hard, places and people are ready for change. There can often be a feeling of hopelessness. People frequently flee in times of trouble, but those that stay find the assets that matter most. Cities that have reinvented themselves often do it with a lot less than you'd imagine—by working with exactly what they have to build the places they want to become.

Like OKC, **New Orleans** has overcome an incredible and devastating tragedy that came in the form of a hurricane. That storm could have ruined NOLA forever. Instead, and only because of the city's rich traditions, it revealed the city's strongest legacies and deepest strengths, and unearthed a new spirit of entrepreneurship aimed at bridging their deep social and political divides.

In our next chapter, **"The Best Thing That Never Happened,"** we see that cities can create opportunity even on the heels of major failures or disappointing developments. Cities on the brink of economic free fall get desperate, and the situation in 1980s Oklahoma City was as bad as it gets. Out of nowhere, the opportunity of the century appeared on the horizon: United Airlines announced its intent to build a major new facility in some lucky city in the United States. Though that vision failed, it was what OKC did after our crushing defeat that has set our city on a new course to the future.

In much the same way, our story from **Seattle** and their failure to build "next-generation" nuclear power sources paved the way to a commitment to sustainability that has become that city's brand. And built an approach to powering a city that has spread across the country, and around the globe.

In **"Government We Want to Pay For,"** we see that even in deep red Republican territory like Oklahoma, public leadership can still accomplish the biggest projects and achieve the best results. Conservatives and Republicans have a habit of lambasting government every chance they get. But when elected leaders and their bosses, the taxpayers, have a clear vision and keep their priorities straight, there is no better tool in the box than government.

In **Albuquerque**, Mayor Richard Berry understood how government could focus on its core competencies and power to convene to give its neediest citizens a credible pathway out of poverty. His project to offer an honest day's work for an honest day's wage has reinvented addressing homelessness in his city and many others.

In **"From Mow to Row,"** we see that even areas that have been ignored or seem past their prime can rise to greatness again. The new middles of America are full of stories of reinvention. Reinvented lives, people, neighborhoods, and urban business models. At the end of these stories of change, we see something great—amazing new assets you can't imagine a city being without.

In **Des Moines**, we learn the story of a small foundation that saw a big opportunity in one of the city's historic buildings—and a way to connect Iowa's bright future to its legacy and leaders from the past. We often try to leave our legacies behind as we look to the future—and the story of historic strengths fueling growth and innovation in central Iowa is a path many other cities should travel.

In **"Making the Big Leagues,"** we see that competitive spirit come alive, not just on the basketball court, but in the boardroom and at the negotiating table. There exists in America a list of upper-echelon metros that matter. It is not the biggest cities, the oldest, or the most prosperous. And the list doesn't exist on the front page of a newspaper or deep inside any economics textbook—it is in the ESPN scroll across the bottom of your TV screen. Success in the business of sports is often a game-changer for a city's future. Professional sports matter, and the lengths cities will go to to join the pro sports club, or stay in it, are remarkable. But there are good ways to get that done, and then there are better ways.

Around the same time that Oklahoma City was learning that lesson, Kevin Johnson overcame near-impossible odds to keep a National Basketball Association team—the Kings—in **Sacramento**. Mayor Johnson was the perfect leader for the job, and the team and its new arena are the centerpiece of California's capital city renaissance, which is continuing to pick up steam.

In **"Where Leaders Come From,"** we see that a city can build its own leaders, especially when we let leaders that rise up naturally blaze their own pathways. The important question is: Where do the best people come from, and how do we keep them as they grow? In my experience, the best leaders come from the least likely places. Their résumés might not be littered with fancy degrees and they might not have some impressive pedigree to boast about, but these are the people who will transform the places they want to call home. You will meet Christy Counts in OKC, who could have done anything, lived anywhere, and succeeded in anything she tried, and who chose to use her talent to answer the cries of a needy population that every city has and very often ignores.

Buffalo has an unlikely leader of its own. Pat Whalen could have lived out his years on a ski slope, a life many of us would envy. But his return to work, and the application of his unique entrepreneurial spirit, is changing the tide of growth and opportunity in some incredibly clever ways.

In **"Putting the City on a Diet,"** we see how a city can

tackle a seemingly impossible issue by confronting it with openness and energy. The problem of obesity was real in Oklahoma City for a generation, but somehow we couldn't see it, and we definitely did not want to talk about it. One day I looked down at the scale, and I saw clearly that I was a part of the problem, too. What we decided to do about it was harder than it sounds—and had a bigger impact than I ever expected: We started an honest conversation about our weight and our health, and our city has never been the same.

Louisville mayor Greg Fischer's work to improve his city, too, has grown from a place of openness: a conversation about mindfulness and meditation that has led to real change in how life works in Louisville.

In **"Building for the Future,"** we see just how fast a change can take hold. In a period of just a few years, Oklahoma City's downtown was reinvented from literally the least walkable in the nation to a district on the cutting edge of connectivity, walkability, and community innovation. This change required big ideas, aligned leaders, and significant investment. But it really began when we started looking at our city through the eyes of the people who live there.

As these kinds of changes take hold in my city, and maybe yours, we must look to the modern history of **Chattanooga**. A generation ago, that city reinvented its downtown, and today it continues that reinvention, extending the impact of change by investing in people as much as place.

And finally, in **"Punching Above Our Weight,"** we see just how far this vision of growing small cities and strong small towns can go. In towns of ten thousand and cities of one million, the tools of the trade are very much the same. The biggest ideas can come from some of the smallest places—and as technology connects communities, the size at which global impact and local meaning can flourish is getting smaller and smaller. I learn this every summer on my vacations around the Midwest, when I drive from small town to small town, taking it all in. There's something magical about a town of ten thousand that has kept it together and found a way to grow despite all the challenges they face. And while many of Oklahoma's small towns are flourishing, the biggest lesson I've learned about what makes a city strong came to me along a stretch of Highway 82 on the road to **El Dorado, Arkansas**.

As any mayor will tell you, there's not much you can do on your own—no matter the size of the city you lead. In the finest example of a mayor I know, the story of Mayor Joe Riley, and his forty-year tenure in **Charleston**, makes plain just what makes any mayor, and the unique connections we make, a critical piece of our nation's success.

Join me on this journey across the country and into the next American city.

CHAPTER 1

Building a City, Beyond Boom and Bust

n 1564, Queen Elizabeth addressed her anxious subjects in
Cambridge and reminded them that "Rome was not built in a
day." I don't know much about the circumstances of her address or why she quoted this grand idea from playwrights and
proverbs, but I know the feeling of needing to stiff-arm detractors
and buy some time on big, slow-moving projects. Whatever she
was up to, it apparently worked, because she reigned over a prosperous and increasingly powerful nation for another forty years.

And of course, the adage is correct: Great nations, grand
cities, or big ideas are generally not built in a day. Rome wasn't.
Neither was New York or any other place, with one notable
exception. Oklahoma City.

On April 22, 1889, as every school kid in Oklahoma knows,
the United States government prepared to hold its first ever
Land Run. The idea of free land was appealing to thousands
from all across America. And so they came. On horseback. By
train. By foot.

The pioneers that had come before were headed west to
California in search of gold and riches. When those fifty thousand souls arrived for the Land Run in 1889, they found a

pretty barren stretch of land on the eastern edge of the western plains. Water was scarce. Trees were few. But the dirt was fertile and the land was free. And that would be enough.

The goal was to settle the Unassigned Lands of Indian Territory, fulfilling the national vision of Manifest Destiny. As kids would today for an Easter egg hunt, people lined up along an imaginary line. A cannon was fired, and they roared across the countryside. By nightfall, ten thousand people were camping in a brand-new town they called Oklahoma City. I maintain that it remains the first city ever to be built in a day.

Welcome to organized chaos. Oklahoma City was strategically located as an urban hub inside a larger area where farms and ranches would be born overnight. In the Land Run, the first person to place a stake to an unclaimed quarter section of land laid claim to the title. These were desperate people, intent on making new lives for themselves. They were entrepreneurs and outlaws. Men and women. Young and old. Mostly poor. Disputes over land popped up everywhere, and the lawmen and judges assigned to create order did the best they could.

To this day, historians debate how the events of that single day continue to shape the soul of Oklahoma City and our state as a whole. I like to think that our origin story instilled a sense of optimism in us. It's a lot easier to think anything's possible when your city was built overnight. And to this day, Oklahoma City residents are always willing to bet on the future. On the other hand, our pioneering spirit brought with it an outsize willingness to chase opportunity, wherever it might be.

Less than two decades after that first Land Run, Oklahoma had become a state. Oklahoma City had become a fully developed city, and the people of Oklahoma voted to make the state's namesake its capital, too.

By then, the markers of our early economic cycle had

begun. Oklahomans were living off the land and were tying their fortunes to commodities. First, it was the price of cotton. Later, the price of wheat. And ultimately, the price of oil and natural gas. Well, what happens when an economy is based around a single commodity? The larger economy rises and falls with that single price. So in Oklahoma and Oklahoma City, the twentieth century became a series of booming economies and fast growth, followed by periods of economic depression and people on the move.

The city and state grew rapidly into the late 1920s. Growth meant more people, more jobs, and more wealth. The city was only forty years old but had become a boom town with millionaires and skyscrapers. Then, the good times ended. The economic depression that affected the entire country destroyed Oklahoma City's economy as well. In rural Oklahoma, clouds of dust destroyed farms and lives. Oklahoma City's businesses and political leaders failed to diversify.

Over the next few years, many of those that were able to leave left. America found other boom towns and people migrated away. Many loaded up the truck, found Route 66, and went west to California. Maybe the millionaires didn't leave, but many of their children did. The city's population shrank and its wealth dissipated. From 1930 to 1970, the U. S. population grew a staggering 65 percent. Meanwhile, Oklahoma's population grew only about 7 percent. In the 1930s and 1940s, Oklahoma had nine members in the U.S. House of Representatives. By the early 2000s, it had five.

Oklahoma City had lost its place among America's elite cities. As its wealth departed, so did its attention to style and appreciation of architecture. Over time, city leaders and city planners embraced sprawl. The city expanded to cover six hundred square miles. And downtown began to die.

Through the years and beyond our first major experiences with boom and bust, however, Oklahoma City remained a hub of optimism and innovation. Early aviators like Wiley Post and Will Rogers were grabbing attention from around the world. The shopping cart was invented in Oklahoma City. And, believe it or not, the parking meter was invented here, too. You are welcome, America!

The point, though, is that even through times of declining growth, or downright depression, people and places like my hometown can find their sense of self. Even if there are bigger lessons left to be learned.

A Prosperity Built on Scarcity

The boom times returned in the 1970s. A strange series of international events created prosperity for us. On the other side of the globe in the Middle East, the petroleum producing nations had created a cartel (OPEC) and made an effort to increase the price of a barrel of oil. It worked. They announced an embargo. The price shot up dramatically—and the repercussions set off a series of events that drove Oklahoma's economy upward.

The nation was gripped by a fear that the United States had lost control of its energy future. There were lines at gas stations. Some cities across the country were even canceling Christmas light displays to cut down on electricity. The energy industry responded with a business model based on that fear and scarcity.

While President Jimmy Carter was wearing a sweater around the White House, watching the thermostat and telling Americans we were running out of oil and natural gas, industry leaders all knew consumption would continue growing in the long run. And in the short run, going along with that feeling of scarcity could create the profits of a lifetime. As a result, the price of oil kept going up and up. And for nearly a decade, Oklahoma's energy-based economy got better and better.

Adding fuel to the fire, several of the nation's biggest banks became eager to get involved in the mania—and most of Oklahoma's bankers were equally eager to take their money. Against inflated global prices, our local bankers would loan the outsiders' cash to Oklahoma oilmen, who bought larger and larger oil rigs and drilled deeper and deeper wells. A few savvy business leaders knew it was an unsustainable business model. Price fluctuates; it doesn't go up and up forever. But that line of thinking was held by people who were in the minority. Most continued to drill and let the rising price of oil fuel the insanity.

Finally, in the spring of 1982, prices began to retreat. Was it a momentary setback or the beginning of the end? The answer came suddenly on July 5.

The first domino to fall was Penn Square Bank. Physically, it was a small bank in a suburban shopping center. It didn't look very imposing but it was beginning to play a larger and larger role in the energy-based economy. The bank's lending principles were highly questionable. It was almost like if you had a pulse, you could get a loan. From across the country, hundreds of millions of dollars had been flowing through the bank and into the Oklahoma oilfields. And as the cost of drilling rose, the bank made bigger and bigger loans until the size of the loan topped the potential revenue from the well. Shockingly, a number of those deals were soon upside down.

The Federal Deposit Insurance Corporation (FDIC) is the federal agency that provides oversight for the banking industry.

FDIC regulators set up an office in the basement of Penn Square Bank and began to examine the financial records. They discovered that sometimes the borrower had not even signed the note. Sometimes the same money was lent to several different people. The bank examiners were aghast and chose to close Penn Square Bank.

Closing even a single bank at first seemed like an overreaction. Bank closings were relatively new to that generation of Americans. Banks had failed across the nation in the 1930s but that seemed like a distant memory to the bankers of 1982. And yet, the other dominoes fell quickly. By the end of the 1980s, over two hundred Oklahoma banks had failed. *Two hundred!*

Oklahoma's economy began to retreat. Ours was a state that had invested most of its dollars in oil and gas, and that industry now seemed on the brink of collapse. As the energy loans failed, we lost virtually all of our banking institutions. As a result, companies in and out of the energy industry started laying people off. Office buildings without workers have a hard time making rents, so the commercial real-estate market took a nosedive. You get the picture. We lost our banks. We lost jobs. We lost our real estate market. And for the second time in a century, we lost people.

We still had our hospital staff and schoolteachers—which every city needs. But, the companies and jobs that *could* move proved harder to hang on to. It seemed like only a few people with the option to go somewhere else stayed. Without much attention from the national media, Oklahoma's economy in the 1980s had become eerily similar to the nation's economy during the Great Depression.

One interesting aspect of an economic depression is when you are going through it, you do not know how long it will last. Every year it seemed like there was a sense we had bottomed out. But 1983 was worse than 1982. And 1984 was worse than 1983. We didn't really know it then, but the bottom finally came in 1987.

By then, the damage was done. We probably had the worst economy in the nation. There didn't seem to be any easy way out. Ten years earlier, the nation's largest banks had been pouring investment dollars into the state. But now, they wanted nothing to do with us. In fact, the thought of investing in Oklahoma conjured up images of a Ponzi scheme. We were an economic pariah. If you are a poor state and you can't attract outside capital, there aren't many options.

A Lost Generation of Leaders and Opportunities

The worst consequence of economic crash might just have been our lost generation of leadership. Perhaps the scale of departures held no candle to the mass migrations of the Dust Bowl and the Great Depression, but the repercussions would turn out to last just as long.

In the 1970s I graduated from a large overachieving public high school called Putnam City. It's not the name of a town, just the name of an independent school district in the middle-class suburbs of Oklahoma City. At Putnam City, we were winning more than our share of athletic championships and more than our share of academic awards. On graduation day, 960 kids had earned a degree.

The sixty highest-performing students wore an orange robe signifying that they had graduated with a grade point average of 4.0 or higher. In a school of high achievement, these were the highest achievers. More than forty years later, I look at the class picture and wonder where those sixty kids are today.

I recognize a handful as Oklahoma City citizens, but the vast majority have moved away.

When you think through the timeline, it is easy to see why these students are not around to enjoy Oklahoma City in the twenty-first century. After leaving Putnam City, these were the kids that went on to get advanced degrees. By the time they graduated college in the 1980s, the economy in Oklahoma had sunk. There were no jobs available that measured up to their educational attainment. Today, those high achievers are in Dallas or Houston or New York or Tokyo. They might be in your town but, for the most part, they are not in mine. It's a shame: We didn't lose them because they wanted to leave, they simply didn't have much of a choice. And this was just at one school. Multiply the Putnam City experience by the number of high schools in Oklahoma City and you have found our lost generation.

In keeping with our pioneering spirit, business leaders and elected officials did make valiant efforts to resurrect the economy. They looked at hosting a world's fair and asked voters to build a large sports stadium to secure big events. Such ideas failed miserably. Voters were not convinced we were up to the task anymore.

Not only could Oklahoma City leadership not pass proactive initiatives to improve the economy, they couldn't even pass routine bond issues to keep our basic infrastructure in decent shape. The streets were bad. Many of the school buildings looked like creepy production sets from horror movies.

In 1984, we learned that our largest sporting event—the National Finals Rodeo—was leaving for Las Vegas. Soon, Oklahoma City University announced it was dropping its sports teams from Division I to the NAIA level. We became the largest city in the country without Division I basketball. Not long after that, our minor-league baseball team was also looking for an exit strategy. Couldn't really blame them.

In a city that had seen plenty of tough times, this seemed like the toughest. In the summer of 1986, the city failed to pass a sales tax election to fund basic services. A month later, the largest financial institution in the state—First National Bank—was closed by the FDIC.

Downtown, the owners of the historic Skirvin Hotel, which had been built in 1910, would soon close its doors and board up the windows. Across the city, hotel and motel occupancy rates were below 30 percent, the lowest in the nation.

Without knowing it, we had reached rock bottom. On the cusp of our city's centennial, 1987 would bring an election to choose a new mayor. It didn't seem like a job anyone would want. There were even more troubling times ahead for our city. Tragedy the likes of which our city—and our nation, to that point—could not yet imagine. But through generations of boom and bust, and surviving tragedies that drew us closer together, we gathered the strength we needed to embrace change and build a better future.

Over the next two decades we would learn a great deal about ourselves, how Oklahoma was viewed by the world, and more importantly, what we believed about ourselves. We learned how to invest in ourselves and, we hope, finally escape that cycle of boom and bust that had dominated our fortunes for a century. In essence, we needed a new worldview and way of building the city we wanted to become. We needed a new rhythm. And I think we found it.

NEW ORLEANS: THE RHYTHM AND RITUAL
OF CITY STRENGTH

Every city has its own identity, and some have even established a unique "brand." A few have gone a layer deeper and figured out what their core values are, whether or not they are noted in any official way. Then there is an upper echelon of places that have a unique character known around the world. New York is one of those cities. But I learned—over many weekends spent in the West Village studying for my MBA at New York University—that even the biggest city in the world is, in the end, made up of distinct neighborhoods with their own voice and brand.

One of the key questions city leaders across the country are wrestling with is this: How can a place that isn't nearly big enough to be a global force on its size alone create an identity known around the world?

Put another way, how can smaller cities grow not only physically but, let's say, *spiritually* as well? This kind of civic strength is important for much deeper reasons than mere economic growth. After the devastating attacks we suffered in 1995, Oklahoma City had to dig deep into the wells of strength we had dug while building jobs and companies and sidewalks—and that is what gave my city what it needed to recover, and to improve.

Brands are great for cities, but personalities are better. And the personality of a place grows from a city's history, and informs a city's posture toward the present and future. On that front, I think there is no city on earth with as distinct a spirit as the Big Easy.

This is a pretty funny nickname for a city like New Orleans. Living there, or even just visiting, is not always the easiest thing to do. Visitors often fight against throngs of crowds, struggle to find parking, and get more than a little confused by the layout of streets in the French Quarter and beyond. And it's hot. But it all seems to add to the city's charm, and people keep coming, year after year, season after season, for one of a dozen or so incredible events and festivals that can only call that city home.

As locals tell it, you can admire New Orleans from afar, but it's not possible to understand or learn to love the place until you've lived there for a time. New Yorkers measure this rite of passage in years. Most people seem to say it's about a decade before you've paid your dues and can adopt the Big Apple as your new hometown. In New Orleans, it might be better to measure this out in seasons. Or as Tim Williamson, CEO of the NOLA Media Group, publisher of *The Times-Picayune*, puts it: "Until you've grown to understand how the cadence of seasons and holidays tells the city's story."

Tim Williamson is probably one of the smartest people I've ever talked to about cities. In a couple of hours of chatting with him, and in several years of working with New Orleans mayor Mitch Landrieu, I learned more about "urban innovation" and "placemaking" and "city resilience" than I could fit between the covers of this book. My notes from those chats are fast and furious, so I probably could never resurface all the wisdom— but I'll say two things about what I did learn.

First, terms like "placemaking" and "urban innovation" are useful, but they are mere husks for the tangible ways each individual place expresses those values for itself. The specifics vary immensely from place to place, and copying another's attempt will get you about as far as the cities vying to be "the next Silicon Valley" have gotten.

Second, most of the time the wisdom at the bottom of that

kind of reflection is impossible to put into a few words, like a slogan or a catchphrase. But Tim Williamson, a New Orleans native who moved away in his twenties and returned home in his thirties, has come about as close as anyone I know to doing so.

Williamson put the distinctiveness of the Big Easy like this: "New Orleans is a city of rhythms and rituals that connects the present to the past, and allows us to view our incredible diversity as a strength that no place in the world can match."

From Mardi Gras in early spring to Jazz Fest just a few weeks later, from dozens of international summertime events to the autumn prestige and pageantry of football season and homecoming, the march of life makes New Orleans what it is.

How Disasters Uncover Your City's Strengths

In the wake of the bombing of the Alfred P. Murrah Federal Building in April 1995, the eyes of the world were, perhaps for the first time in history, trained on Oklahoma City. We weren't used to the attention, and I remember how much we wished the world would look away. In the aftermath of the hurricane that hit New Orleans ten years later, I remember thinking about all the residual effects of a disaster that affected not just one single block or building downtown.

And how different—not better or worse, but different—it must have felt that the pain was caused by an act of God as opposed to an attack by a few men. At some point, the people of New Orleans probably wanted the world to look away as well, but for different reasons than we did.

NOLA is accustomed to attention. New Orleanians seem to revel in it, and every couple of months a new part of the city's calendar kicks in. But this was attention that the city did not want, though every ounce of help that attention brought was needed.

Hurricane Katrina did more than reveal a weak set of levees or a strained decision-making mechanism that had allowed much of the city to live in danger for so long. It also revealed that much of the city's public leadership was weak where it needed to be stronger. And where help was needed most, the storm uncovered the residue of a corrupt and decaying bureaucracy.

A bit too late, the city was called to evacuate, sparking traffic and panic that in some ways caused more harm than good. Those that could get out were separated from their city and their homes and their loved ones. Those that were trapped suffered life-threatening isolation.

The images are still fresh in my mind; perhaps they are in yours as well. Not just days later, but weeks, even years, after the storm passed we were all rightly worried about whether that magical place could ever recover. Would the thousands of refugees who'd ended up in Houston and Dallas and my city and dozens of others ever return?

It was no sure thing. The threat that New Orleans would be forever crippled was real. Would there be a Mardi Gras in 2006? Would Jazz Fest, like the Hornets and the Saints, need to find another place to soldier on?

This is where the story gets good—and where Tim's ideas of rhythm and ritual really hit home for me. New Orleans got back on its feet *precisely because* of the sense of purpose that comes from the city's diverse traditions. And despite the depth of the devastation of the storm, it happened right away.

Though the official leadership had been eroded for decades, and institutions, especially schools and government, were in states of terrible disrepair, a group of leaders stepped up and set their minds to restarting the calendar and putting the rituals of New Orleans life back into place.

Tim Williamson is one of those people. In the years before the storm, he had returned from building his career in Boston and several other cities where he learned a lot about what other places had to offer—how things could be different, and better. He had returned home with an idea about how to make his city a better place.

What he says about his return, and those of several others who came back in their thirties and forties around the same time, was that they didn't return for opportunity. "In the '80s and '90s, you didn't come back to build your career. There weren't any great companies or big jobs here. What we came home for was the love of our city and our connection to the place itself."

Pulled by the traditions and culture of the city, that set of young professional leaders had returned just in time to do their part in rebuilding the foundations that Katrina had threatened to wash away forever.

Today New Orleans is booming again. Business is back and jobs are growing. There are still serious physical and social infrastructure problems to fix. But you can hardly head to a conference on cities without a great speaker showing up on the stage to describe some facet of the new and creative work that is under way. And you can scarcely find one of "the lists" on entrepreneurship or innovation where New Orleans isn't in the mix.

There's something particularly important about what's happening with the growth of entrepreneurship and creativity in New Orleans as well. Just as with the return to Middle American cities like my own and dozens more, New Orleans is experiencing a dramatic influx of top talent drawn to the opportunity to be a part of the city's rebuilding years. Williamson's own project, The Idea Village, started with a handful of other New Orleanians returning home, and is flanked by new and exciting organizations like Andrea Chen's non-profit Propeller, New Orleans Entrepreneurship Week, and new initiatives at old institutions like Tulane University. This mix of natural strengths under the guidance of new NOLA leaders like Tulane's Rob Lalka is combining to create bold solutions to generational problems that the old approaches proved unable to solve.

What made the difference between total devastation and the dramatic comeback we have witnessed was the buoyancy of spirit that the citizens of New Orleans had built throughout the city's history—and which its leaders and residents rely on when they need it most. And for your city, when tough times come, the young professionals and workers who live there, whether they have come for new opportunities or have returned simply for the love they feel for home, are the best asset you could ever hope to have.

CHAPTER 2

The Best Thing That Never Happened

Things were bleak in Oklahoma City. Offices sat vacant. Downtown was deserted and school buildings were being shuttered. Workers were fleeing the city by the thousands, while somehow our unemployment hovered at nearly twice the national average. The real price of a gallon of gas was at its lowest in our nation's history. And while that might sound like good news for millions of drivers, when your economy is built on oil, nothing could be worse. But the year wasn't 1929 and this wasn't the Dust Bowl.

It was the '80s in Oklahoma City. In Ronald Reagan's two terms as president, the economy grew by over 30 percent and more than 16 million jobs were created. In the national headlines, the progress sure seemed to be real, but in OKC, it was more like the recovery that wasn't.

So, whether or not Ron Norick was looking for a challenge, he found it. In 1987, at the age of forty-five, he was elected mayor of Oklahoma City. There were certainly celebrations and inspired victory speeches. But in truth, the mood did not match the rhetoric. And for Oklahomans, memories of the Great Depression were not so far off in the rearview mirror.

As Norick took office, the city's economy had been sinking for five years. It was among the worst in the nation by many measures. Especially given the outsize local impact of the national banking collapse, it was *the* worst. By then, over two hundred banks across the state had failed. Imagine the devastation, a state the size of Oklahoma having two hundred banks fail to meet their obligations.

The oil and gas industry had been the foundation of our economy, even through the low cycles in which our economy was decimated by falling prices. A barrel of oil, once $40, had fallen to $10. The oil and gas industry, banking, and real estate were all at rock bottom.

On top of it all the mayor's job, a part-time gig that consumes far more energy and time than your average full-time job, paid a whopping $2,000 a year. Welcome to city hall, Mr. Norick!

Since the 1930s, Oklahoma City has always had a city manager who ran city government on a day-to-day basis. The manager sees that we have first responders on duty. He or she is responsible for the trash, the water, the airport, the parks, you name it. The mayor and council meet one morning a week and serve as a board of directors. The mayor is essentially the chairman of the board. The city manager is essentially the CEO. None of this is easy. But when the world is falling apart (and that's kind of how it seemed at city hall in the 1980s), it is difficult to pull people together and lead a city toward a better tomorrow. And by the way, things were not getting better anytime soon.

Norick probably knew what he was getting into. In the late 1950s and early 1960s, his father had been on the city council and served two terms as a popular mayor. Through that experience, Ron grew up knowing more about Oklahoma City politics than most. But it would be wrong to think of the Noricks as a political dynasty, and political victories would not necessarily come naturally to Ron. The Noricks were businessmen. They owned and operated a printing company. They weren't politicians in the traditional sense.

Norick was part of the city's esteemed leadership and was well respected by the business community, but he also understood what the working man and woman thought, and what they wanted. Picking up on these instincts, he ran for office on a platform of creating jobs. Well, no argument there—not from anyone. That's what Oklahoma City needed. But how, everyone wondered, do you turn around an economy that is in free fall?

Mayor Norick came to city hall and looked at the city budget like a businessman. He saw that too many decisions and expenditures were made in the context of crisis. Because revenue was declining, city managers were doing all they could to get to the next week, the next day. There was no investing in the future. They weren't building new streets because they could barely fill potholes in the streets that already existed. And the insidious thing about that kind of stop-gap approach is that it all but guarantees the situation will get even worse. Even in those dark days, Oklahoma City became known as one of the best-run cities in the country. Norick stopped the budget hemorrhaging, modernized our basic systems, and put the books back on track. But stopping the bleeding would not be enough and he knew it.

Facing a tough pitcher and holding a cracked bat, Norick chose to swing for the fences.

The Deal of the Century: United Airlines

When news started spreading in the business community that United Airlines was looking around the country for a site to build a new maintenance facility, Mayor Norick decided to act. He knew it wouldn't be easy. This was the big one. This new facility would create as many as seven thousand great new jobs. The annual economic impact to a local community would be nearly a billion dollars. Holy cow! This could be Oklahoma City's answer.

Over one hundred cities around the country were bidding on the project but none were as desperate as us. And no elected official was as committed to hitting the home run as Mayor Norick.

Today, cities have all sorts of complex and creative ways of putting together incentive packages to attract new businesses. States typically have some legislation in place that allows elected officials to lower a company's tax bill and encourage hiring local workers without putting taxpayers at an unfair risk. With these tools, cities compete against each other for creative deals that benefit both sides. Most of the incentives are performance based: Bring us the jobs and we'll lower your taxes or cost of doing business, that kind of thing.

But in 1987, at least in Oklahoma City, there weren't many options to create a competitive advantage. Norick, however, knew what CEOs of big companies were thinking. Mayor Norick was probably the one guy who could get OKC a serious look. CEOs liked him; and he spoke their language.

Knowing that he needed to let United Airlines understand his level of commitment, Norick explained that he was going to ask his voters to pass a penny-on-the-dollar sales tax for three years. The tax would generate around $120 million and would be used to help construct the facility for United.

When word of Oklahoma City's plan reached corporate headquarters in Chicago, there was disbelief. They smiled and wished Norick well with his election but they were pretty sure that voters in Oklahoma City were not going to pass such an outrageous initiative as a substantial sales tax to pay for corporate welfare. It sounded too good to be true.

But United's leadership underestimated Oklahoma City's level of desperation. And they underestimated the mayor. Norick told the citizens of Oklahoma City, and the entire county, that this would be the catalyst the local economy needed. And the people trusted him. The measure passed with 62 percent of the vote. On the news, citizens cheered with delight, believing that some good news was finally on the horizon.

Meanwhile, United Airlines officials in Chicago were shocked. The mayor had pulled it off. Obviously, they were going to have to put Oklahoma City on the short list.

Sensing some momentum and trying to close the deal, Norick then worked with Oklahoma governor David Walters to increase the incentive package with state dollars. Walters called a special session of the legislature—which is unheard of—and he got it approved. The total incentive package was now reportedly weighing in at over $300 million.

Whatever the final amount would have been, it was money we didn't really have—and definitely didn't need to be stuffing in the pockets of United Airlines executives. But at the time, we were desperate for jobs. And willing to do whatever it took to get them.

Now usually, economic development deals are executed behind the scenes. The media and general public don't really tune in to stories on tax abatements. But because of the sales-tax election and the legislature's special session, this effort gained a high profile. It generated front-page headlines, and even led the ten o'clock news.

To put it mildly, expectations were high.

Decision day finally neared. United called all of the competing cities into Chicago for a final round of negotiations. One more chance to make a pitch. Then, United's board of directors made a decision and Ron Norick got the phone call.

The facility would be built in . . . Indianapolis.

The Kick in the Teeth We Needed

Whatever oxygen was left was promptly sucked out of the room. We'd been under the impression that we were going to get the facility. We were expecting the validation of having a huge company say yes to Oklahoma City. Then we lost and we were stunned by the impact of one more punch in the gut. The television media carried the announcement live. Local reporters who had traveled to Chicago for the announcement now relayed the devastating news back to a disappointed Oklahoma.

Norick was deflated. He had spent over a year of his life on the effort to attract United Airlines. He had used his valuable political capital to pass the sales tax that now wouldn't be enacted. In what had become a very public effort, Norick had swung for the fences and struck out. The negativity that permeated Oklahoma had one more reason to grow.

What interests me most in studying Norick's leadership is not the failed initiative, though. What interests me is what happened next. Norick didn't lie low and lick his wounds. He didn't take a long vacation. Instead, Norick continued conversations with United. He wanted to understand. *Where did we go wrong?*

United's initial response was dismissive. They didn't see a need to get into the details of their evaluation. "Mayor, you were the most prepared. The most courteous. You were prompt with your proposals. No hard feelings, let's all just move on."

But Norick didn't give up. He pushed for an answer from United on their decision-making process. How could Oklahoma City learn from the experience if we didn't get some answers?

Finally, United came clean. It turned out, unbeknownst to our local leaders, United had sent a handful of mid-level executives and their spouses to downtown Oklahoma City to spend a weekend. When the group reported back to headquarters and that report made its way to the board of directors, Oklahoma City's effort was doomed. The incentive package didn't matter anymore.

The airport might be a wonderful place to fix their fleet of aircraft. The problem was the place. United's employees just couldn't imagine living here.

Mayors of Oklahoma City are gluttons for pain, and this was the kick in the teeth that the mayor needed.

This information forced city leaders to confront the issue that had been staring them in the face the entire time. The quality of life in Oklahoma City had sunk so low that we could no longer buy the allegiance of corporate America. We were in denial about just how bad things had gotten. Wealthy people had moved away from the city center out to the far reaches of Oklahoma City. Living their suburban lives, they weren't forced to see what the United execs saw when they visited.

Downtown was dead. Sure, there were still some jobs in the tall buildings. But at exactly five o'clock, people hit the road. They got in their cars and flew down the one-way streets to the on-ramps and the interstate highways, and made the twenty-minute ride to their homes, or the mall, or to pick their kids up at school.

By five-thirty you could have fired off a cannon downtown and nobody would have noticed. The neighborhoods, schools, and shopping malls to which workers retreated had become the lifeblood of our "urban" life. This had not always been the case. Downtown Oklahoma City had once been a booming, cosmopolitan place. In the first half of the twentieth century, it had been full of restaurants and movie theaters and hotels. It had been the center of town and the center of activity.

Not too long after United's news, Norick took a trip and found himself in downtown Indy. What he saw there changed the course of history in OKC.

You Can't Be a Suburb of Nothing

In Indianapolis, Mayor Norick got a good look at "the competition." Downtown Indy had something we didn't. There were sports arenas and water projects. There were new hotels, cranes in the sky, and a lot of restaurants. Perhaps strangest of all: People actually lived downtown. At that time if someone said they lived in downtown Oklahoma City, you could almost guess they were in the county jail.

Norick realized that Indy was on the other side of a paradigm shift in economic development. Oklahoma City had missed it. Like many governments still do today, we were trying to "create jobs." We thought if we could create jobs, we would attract people. If we could have landed the opportunity with United Airlines, people would have moved to the city for a job. We had it backward. Businesses create jobs. *Governments and public servants build places.*

Indianapolis had figured out that if you could create a place that people wanted to live, people would move there. The jobs would come to you. But it hadn't always been that way in Indianapolis, either.

The 1970s and 1980s were tough times in urban America. During the depths of the pre-Reagan recession and the gas crisis, cities across the country were in a state of despair. Especially in the Midwest, the economy was struggling, crime was on the rise, blue-collar jobs were moving to the suburbs or overseas, and racial tensions were rising fast. America's central business districts were hollowing out, and our cities were in a frightening state of decline.

Indianapolis saw a path forward before many, many others had cracked the code. And a series of visionary mayors helped to make that change happen.

First came Richard Lugar, who took office at the height of America's cultural tumult in 1968. Most of us in politics know Mr. Lugar as Indiana's great senator and foreign policy expert. But before he went to Washington, Mayor Lugar brought his city, county, and region together under a creative consolidated government called Unigov. In truth, the genius of this idea is one of the biggest untapped opportunities for driving change in local government. We tried it in Oklahoma City and failed. There's no question in my mind that Unigov put Indianapolis ahead in the game. It definitely set the stage for the second great mayor in modern Indianapolis history.

After Mayor Lugar, a mild-mannered divinity student and Presbyterian minister took the top job at city hall. Building on his predecessor's work to unite the city and county, Mayor Bill Hudnut did something unthinkable in cities at that time—he pointed attention, and time, and capital to the metro's deserted downtown. The social and economic forces that were driving

51

people, jobs, and opportunity to the suburbs and exurbs in those years were enormously powerful.

Mayor Hudnut's inimitable legacy is that he believed a city, its leaders, and citizens could create new value and positive change. Most of his colleagues in city halls at that time seemed satisfied to manage an inevitable, long, and painful decline. In the words of David Gogol, one of his longtime advisors, "Hudnut's most important legacy was to convince the city that it didn't need to be a victim of societal and economic changes. It could fight these forces. And win."

Hudnut's vision was as ingenious as it was clear. "You Can't Be a Suburb of Nothing." *Pastor* Hudnut was truly a voice in the wilderness.

In his sixteen years as mayor, William Hudnut's leadership transformed Indianapolis from just another city with another empty downtown into a true global city in the center of the country. Two decades before Oklahoma City got it, he understood the power of sports to create community and build a city's brand. Like Oklahoma City, Indianapolis built the Hoosier Dome before they really had a team to play in it—and used public dollars to support the project in a political environment not terribly keen on putting taxpayer dollars to use in this way.

But the big idea was to make Indy into the Amateur Sports Capital of the World. Now, this might make sense to us in a world dominated by media and branding today—but this was a fairly exotic idea back then. At the federal level, the importance of sports as an economic driver had caught on, but convincing industry leaders locally that it made sense would be a different game. Ultimately, it worked, and though you've probably never heard of Mayor Hudnut, no person is more responsible for the changing course of American cities than he was.

Hudnut's work set the stage for his successors Stephen Goldsmith—probably the smartest city innovator alive—and Greg Ballard and Bart Peterson, who I personally learned so much from, and was proud to compete with, during our time as mayors together.

And because I can, I'd just like to point out that four of those five mayors mentioned above were Republicans. Conservative ideas make a big difference in cities, and I hope my party continues to build the attention we pay to growing urban markets across the country.

But the point of the story is what Mayor Norick saw in Indianapolis. He saw a vibrant downtown. And the fruits of a decade of labor that led to our loss of the United facility. And a pathway to Oklahoma City's future.

A Better City—for Us

Corporate America was beginning to understand that it takes a lot of time, effort, and money to train a workforce. As the most sought-after workers began to choose their city based on the quality of life instead of the quality of a job, it made sense to build teams in cities where people wanted to live. A company needs to retain its workforce. You can't afford to have employees leave the company *not* because of dissatisfaction with the company. This is why great cities matter more than ever.

Armed with this new understanding of Oklahoma City's core problem, Norick and the other business leaders in the community charted a new plan. Norick took note of the citizens' willingness to pass a one-penny sales tax for United and considered aloud whether they'd be willing to pass a sales tax increase for themselves. Three years later, Norick was in the middle of a campaign called MAPS, which would define his destiny and cement his legacy.

MAPS stood for "Metropolitan Area ProjectS." And although improving the quality of life in a community can be complicated, MAPS had a lot of simplicity in its design. It was easy to understand. Norick and the city council were asking the voters to pass a one-cent sales tax that would last for five years.

Why five years? Norick figured it was about the amount of time that people used to finance a new family car. Voters could get their heads around the length of the commitment; they could understand it was a pretty fair deal. The other side of things remained pretty simple, too. With the $200 million in revenue that would be created, the city would build nine projects in total.

Some of the projects were high profile. For example, to end the embarrassment of having a dry riverbed downtown, there would be dams constructed to impound water, creating a nearly five-mile waterway. The citizens' general reaction? *Sounds great! Yes, let's put water in the river!*

Another water project required a lot of vision. It also required us to steal an idea from another city. In San Antonio, Texas, there was a tremendous success story of an entertainment district centered around a canal. Oklahoma City's plan would be to build a canal through an abandoned warehouse district with the idea that it could duplicate San Antonio's entertainment district success. The citizens' general reaction? *Are you crazy? In Bricktown? Where all those boarded-up buildings are? That's the dumbest idea I've ever heard!*

Most of the other ideas were more predictable and less controversial:

- A new ballpark so we could keep our AAA baseball team.
- A new sports arena that could maybe someday lure an NHL or NBA team to town.
- A new downtown library.
- Some improvements to our performing arts center and our fairgrounds.
- Some help for our struggling public transit.

Norick also placed all nine parts of the initiative onto one ballot with one up-or-down vote. It was all or nothing. In poker terms, Norick was asking Oklahoma City to go "all in."

This was a critical decision, because the campaign forced different support groups to work together. Those that loved sports were working with those that loved the arts. Library enthusiasts were joining hands with people that were pushing for the water projects. The MAPS election created a vehicle that helped unify the leadership.

So with seemingly everything on the line, the campaign began. The chamber funded the effort. There were TV ads, brochures, and old-fashioned door-knocking. There was no funded opposition but there was plenty of negativity. The city just didn't have a reputation for getting things done. After years of gradually lowering services, they had started to hire more police officers. But build stuff? When was the last time the city built anything worthwhile? It had probably been twenty years! Who would manage the construction? Who would look after all the money? And why were we building all these things downtown? No one wanted to go downtown. Why were we trying to attract people to come here? We didn't want strangers in our town.

"The campaign was going awful," Norick said later.

Finally, as election day neared, Norick spoke to the voters in a way only a plain-speaking man-of-the-people could. "Look," he said. "Even if no one moves here because of MAPS, and even if no one comes here to create a job because of MAPS, the worst-case scenario is this: We will have a better city for us. Wouldn't you like a better city for your kids or your grandkids?"

Some years later I learned a little story that I think says a lot about the kinds of things desperate but dedicated leaders are required to do.

As the campaign was coming together, the chamber of commerce started to get cold feet and worried that they might not go through with the work after all. Mayor Norick was not happy, and threatened that if the deal fell through, he'd end his time as mayor at the next election. The mayor was enormously popular, even if his initiative wasn't. His margin of victory in the previous election had been an incredible 80 percent. Without MAPS, there would still be things to get done. He just didn't want to be the mayor of a city that refused to invest in itself.

Election day arrived and voter turnout was heavy. That night, Norick gathered with friends to watch the media report on the results. His term as mayor had four months remaining. He had already decided if MAPS failed to get the required 50 percent, he would not seek another term. He viewed this election as a reflection on his ability to lead. And if MAPS was not the answer, someone else would need to take over at city hall.

Across town, a volunteer group of naysayers also gathered. And with television cameras rolling, they cheered the early voting results that showed MAPS was trailing 51 percent to 49 percent. "There's trouble in River City," mocked one woman, thrilled with the idea that city hall might fail again. She was apparently satisfied with a river that didn't have any water in it.

Norick was cautiously optimistic but had prepared a concession speech in case it was needed. His campaign team told him that despite the early returns, they were likely to pull out a victory. They had checked some key precincts and felt optimistic. And this time the political scientists were correct.

When the final results came in, MAPS had won: 52 percent to 48 percent.

"Oklahoma City," Norick began as he addressed the enthusiastic crowd, "welcome to the big leagues."

From Worst to First

For the mayor, his city council, and the business leaders of the city, there was vindication ahead. The sting of losing United was fading away. And although the implementation of MAPS would have its share of early issues, it would ultimately transform the community. This may sound like an exaggeration, but it is not: *MAPS changed everything.*

Seven million people a year flock to Bricktown. The canal that seemed like such a silly idea is now one of the greatest investments the city ever made. The Oklahoma City Thunder play basketball in the MAPS-funded arena.

The investment on the river has created the finest venue in the world for the sports of canoe, kayak, and rowing. When MAPS passed, there was one downtown hotel. Today there are nineteen, with several more on the way. Restaurants flourish. Corporate headquarters have been expanded. Six billion dollars of private-sector money has poured into the city, much of it from out of town.

And since that election, the city's economy has improved from perhaps the nation's worst to one of the nation's best. Through the deepest parts of the 2008 housing bubble and economic crisis, an economy that had once suffered terrible losses in downturns continued to flourish and kept its unemployment and foreclosure rates far below the national average.

Keep in mind, it's been twenty-five years since the MAPS election. Norick enjoys retirement. More than half of his city council has died. The business leaders of today are largely of a new generation.

And that United Airlines facility in Indianapolis? It did open in 1994. But employment numbers never even reached half what they were promised. The airline was slated to invest $500 million of its own money into the state's economy, but only ever spent about two-thirds that amount. And in 2002, as United went through bankruptcy, they closed up shop and the hangars sat shuttered for years.

The what-ifs that come to mind are huge. What if we'd put another hundred million on the table and made the airline an offer they couldn't refuse? What if Norick had won?

He would have never been forced to ask the hard questions and look at our city in new ways. He would have never made that trip up to Indy. He never would have launched MAPS. And Oklahoma City might still be a suburb of nothing with a $300 million investment sitting dark out there at the end of an airport runway.

Safe to say, failing to attract United Airlines is the greatest thing that ever happened to our town.

SEATTLE: WPPSS! HOW THE EMERALD CITY'S MISSTEPS CREATED SUSTAINABILITY

I f you've ever been to Seattle, I think you'll know what I mean.
There's just something different about the way that city and nature are intertwined. Part of the magic is how lush and rich the Pacific forest and coastlines remain despite their new neighbor we call "civilization." Part is how the steep downtown streets, carved into a hillside along the Puget Sound, connect you with the light and the water at every sunset.

Things were not always so idyllic in the Emerald City. Like most western cities, Seattle's history is marked by gold rushes and oil booms—and the busts and hard times that seem to always follow them. But in the post-war expansion, Boeing had become the city's anchor. Now, that might seem like a bad analogy to use for an airplane manufacturer, but you'll see the fit shortly.

As the Apollo Program and Vietnam War spending wound down in the late 1960s, so did Boeing's business. Between 1968 and 1971, the company laid off almost sixty thousand workers and ended contracts with hundreds of local suppliers. In response, local businesses shuttered left and right. *City unemployment shot as high as 25 percent.*

The company that once connected the planet with the skies was now dragging its hometown to the bottom of the sound. Halfway as a joke, but capturing the anxiety, a couple of local businessmen paid to install a billboard on the highway between downtown and the airport saying:

**Will the last person leaving Seattle—
turn out the lights.**

Sure, people were leaving—but by the tens of thousands, not the hundreds of thousands. Something about Seattle was making a lot of highly trained engineers and executives stick with their city through the worst of it all. As former mayor Charles Royer put it to me, "Those engineers and scientists were creators. They created industries and machines that changed the world. Instead of running away when times got tough, they worked hard and invented ways to stay. They could have gone anywhere in the world. Seattle had become the place they called home."

They invented ways to stay. What would lead engineers who could land a job in almost any city on the planet to reinvent themselves or take a massive risk and found a new company like this? To be sure, the city's majestic mountain views and profound connection to the water laid the foundation. But there was something more.

And that something more started with a mistake.

You see, in the height of the 1950s and 1960s post-war industrial boom, the city's demographers and planners were wearing some pretty rosy glasses and assumed that their region's growth would continue without interruption for decades to come. Some of those same engineers did the math and came to a simple conclusion: Seattle needed more (and more) power to fuel its incredible growth.

How much power?

Well, the utilities in the Pacific Northwest region figured another forty thousand megawatts of capacity to be exact. That's a lot of electricity. So much that the region could no longer depend upon building more hydroelectric dams to meet the need. Sticking with water for power would destroy the Columbia River Valley's ecosystem—something Seattleites of that generation already understood.

In that sense they were ahead of their time. And in keeping with their modern ways, the plans that the federal government's Bonneville Power Administration cooked up called for a state-of-the-art, next-generation solution to their power fears. Thermal power plants. In particular, *nuclear* power plants. And a lot of them. Things didn't go quite as planned.

Bad Ideas and Worse Acronyms

Governments aren't so good at naming things—especially visionary projects that excite the urbanists but are hard for everyday folks to understand. For example, there are your typical alphabet-soup names for government departments, some of which awkwardly spell out barely related words. Some of them don't have any vowels at all. The whole thing is kind of weird.

So, in the annals of bad government acronyms the Washington Public Power Supply System has sort of gone down in history for being one of the most prescient and unfortunate acronyms. Say it along with me now . . . "Whoops!"

WPPSS is a group of twenty-three public utilities in Washington State that makes sure the region's electrical needs are met. This is an incredibly complex business—the technology and machinery alone are ten levels above my pay grade, to say nothing of the difficulty of designing projects today that won't go into use for five or ten years into the future. Perhaps the words often attributed to Niels Bohr, discoverer of the electron, are fitting here: "It's hard to predict. Especially the future."

The WPPSS built some pretty complex models to guess how many people would live in Washington and the Puget Sound area far into the future. Compounding complex calculations of the region's future population with detailed analyses of the amount of electricity our generations would use started turning out big numbers. Numbers describing the size of future demand for electricity that boggled the mind. Those forty thousand megawatts of power would require twenty coal-fired plants, twenty nuclear power plants, and, for good measure, two new hydropower dams.

To Seattleites and others around the Puget Sound, the whole idea felt a little uncomfortable. They had taken advantage of the powerful Columbia River Valley for their energy needs. But numbers don't lie, or so we're often told, and the only reasonable way to close the forty thousand megawatt gap was hidden inside the nucleus of the atom.

Building nuclear power plants isn't cheap, and with twenty of them in the works, the power authorities and the utility companies would have to get creative. First, they put together a high-wire act that allowed debt to be financed at federal government rates. Then they architected the purchase of those future plants' power across all twenty-three utilities and other groups. Somehow, they found enough money—or, at least, enough to get started.

The initial plans showed plants being built quickly, and power coming online so fast that electricity would be "too cheap to meter." But it didn't quite work out that way. The teams had little experience building nuclear plants, so construction timetables fell apart and building costs soared by 400–500 percent. The delivery of sellable power was delayed significantly but the massive payments to lenders were still coming due. Worst of all, the growth predictions that drove the demand curves? They just weren't coming true.

By the time the plan finally toppled, it had become the biggest municipal bond default in our country's history. Unpayable debts of $2.55 billion had to be worked out. And keep in mind, the entire project was set to cost over ten times that amount after all the plants were complete. To this day, and into the 2030s, Puget Sound residents will pay part of their electric bill for the costs of nuclear plants that couldn't even keep *their own* lights on.

WPPSS!

The Best of the Story: Conserving the City's Future

The litany of mistakes behind WPPSS and its nuclear power foibles are spectacular—and volumes of history have been written about it. The thing to notice here is what leaders in Seattle did as the projects faltered, crumbled, and ultimately failed. Unlike so many leaders today, who rejoice in the failure of the so-called opposition without planning an alternative that lives up to better ideals, Seattleites responded to failure in a fashion that we can learn from today.

Though the writing wasn't exactly on the wall yet, the environmentally minded and cost-conscious city council members and local leaders believed there was a better way to respond to the energy crisis than venturing off into the unknown, or doubling down on risky bets that overambitious advocates of "progress" were recommending so strongly. They believed that a solution to the city's energy crisis could be found in their tried-and-true commitments to conservation and protection of their natural surroundings.

But instincts and platitudes would not be enough. The region's environmentalists needed to develop a plan that would handle the possibility of short-run energy crises, meet the region's long-term need for power, and measure up to the critical eye of economists and accountants at the same time.

In a word, they showed that even in a time of relatively cheap power, the cost of creation outstripped the value of savings and conservation. Basically, they discovered that it was four to five times more expensive to build new power plants than it was to take steps to see that those plants didn't need to be built in the first place.

Early efforts were simply to teach customers that despite the low cost of power, you needed to turn off the lights and other devices if you left a room. The next stage was more around retrofitting electrically heated homes and buildings with more efficient windows and insulation. With cheap electricity and mild weather, no one had considered these steps before.

The nuances of the story are way too detailed (and too full of impenetrable acronyms) to tell the whole tale here. But the upshot for the region has been remarkable. Despite the failure of perhaps the most ambitious construction plan in local government history, Seattle and the surrounding region has remained on the cutting edge of energy innovation—due in large part to their efforts to conserve energy wherever they could.

That spirit of conservation has permeated many areas of work in the Puget Sound. For example, the region's water authority has added almost four hundred thousand new users to their system since 1980, yet the region's annual water usage has dropped by over 30 percent.

For Seattle, the value may best be found in the comments Mayor Royer made at the beginning of this story—about how through the depths of the Boeing Bust the best and brightest "invented ways to stay." I believe this is the place that our cities' distinct values have their strongest impact.

Seattle's resilience comes in part from the way a sunset rolls up the downtown streets. But what really makes the place feel like nirvana to those who call it home is the sense of self and place and the city's unique values that imbue the experience of living there. That's what motivates people to invent ways to stay.

As we in Oklahoma City can be grateful for "The Best Thing That Never Happened" in the United Airlines story, so we as a country have Seattle's mistakes to thank for a major positive change in their city—and in our country as a whole.

CHAPTER 3

Government We Want to Pay For

In deep red territory like Oklahoma, politicians talking about anything that even smells like a tax increase can be a dangerous game. Every county voted for Donald Trump in 2016. And Democrats, even in our largest, most urban districts, are pretty conservative about the use of taxpayer dollars.

So, it's been no easy task for a small-government Republican like me to explain the difference between good taxes and bad taxes, or between wasted dollars and big projects worth the public's support.

While it's easy to look back at Oklahoma City's success and see the wisdom in that vote for a penny-on-the-dollar sales tax, we should take a close look at the ways it was the beginning of all the positive change we continue to see in our city.

First, it kick-started investment in the urban core. Remember, like many others in the country at that time, our downtown was dying. If you were going to build a hotel, you would build it out in the suburbs. If you were going to build a church, you wouldn't have built it downtown because there were no people down there. MAPS changed all this and revitalized the core. A dying downtown was soon the catalyst for a complete urban makeover. Once the city started investing in the downtown area, restaurants started going in and the medical research center expanded.

An initial $300 million public investment led to at least $6 billion in private-sector investment. Even the most ardent, rock-ribbed, small-government conservative has trouble criticizing the method or the results.

Secondly, it created a genuine sense of pride in the city. It seems every city makes an effort to build a place's pride. Even if it's just a public relations campaign or a series of billboards with a catchy slogan, it's better than nothing. But this was real pride. This had substance. People weren't just saying they were proud of their city out of a blind sense of loyalty. They believed it.

The generation of citizens that voted and passed the MAPS initiative take ownership in telling the story. Visitors still recount to me how when they arrived at the airport their taxi driver enthusiastically told them about MAPS and how it changed the city. When your taxi drivers are promoting your city, you've got to be onto something.

Defeating Our Own Worst Enemy

Pride isn't something that comes easily to Oklahomans. Back in the 1930s, Steinbeck's image of the poor, uneducated farmers from *The Grapes of Wrath* inspired embarrassment across the state. And like most stereotypes, there was some truth in that one. There *were* a lot of poor, uneducated people in the state. Of course, there were a lot of poor, uneducated people in all states, but since the Dust Bowl, Oklahomans have been especially sensitive to that characterization. And no mere PR campaign could change that.

In the 1980s, in the midst of a steep economic slump, Oklahoma governor George Nigh hired a British PR firm to do a study on Oklahoma's image. The firm spent months talking to people around the country and around the world about their perceptions of Oklahoma. Finally, the study was complete. Governor Nigh sponsored an event on the campus of the University of Oklahoma, where the results would be revealed. State leaders and the media gathered to hear the news.

"We have searched the entire world and gathered thousands of opinions about Oklahoma," the researcher began. "And we have discovered a negative impression about Oklahoma in only one place."

The speaker paused. And a murmur went through the crowd.

Really? Only one place! The crowd was surprised. They had assumed people around the world had a negative impression of Oklahoma, so this sounded like good news. Maybe our reputation isn't as bad as we thought. By the way, where was this one place? Where was this lone spot on the world map that had a negative impression of our state?

The researcher continued speaking. "The only place where people have a negative impression of Oklahoma is . . . Oklahoma."

We had seen the enemy. And it was us.

Ten years later, MAPS had passed and people were ready to feel optimistic. We all wanted to believe that investing in our city center would change the place, but we didn't have any proof yet. By the beginning of 1995, a year and a half after the

MAPS election, if you looked around downtown, it didn't look that different.

Oklahoma City needed something positive to happen; instead, the worst thing imaginable happened. On April 19, 1995, the largest act of domestic terrorism in United States history occurred in downtown Oklahoma City. A truck bomb exploded at nine o'clock on a Wednesday morning and 168 people were murdered.

The focus of the national and international media was as big as it could have been in those days before ubiquitous cable news. For those weeks, the eyes of the world were on our city. But for all the wrong reasons.

It was a tragedy that struck home. Almost all of the victims had lived in Oklahoma City or the surrounding suburbs. We worked with them. Went to church with them. Their kids went to school with our kids. If you didn't know at least one victim, certainly you knew someone who knew them. It was very personal.

The mourning process was elongated. It took a couple of weeks to find all of the bodies buried in the rubble. So, every day for two weeks, the death toll mounted. Every day there were ten to twenty funerals. In this period of Internet infancy, people still watched television news in large numbers. And the coverage of the bombing was 24/7 for nearly a week. Every day, it seemed like our shoulders slumped just a little bit more.

I think it is important to take a snapshot of Oklahoma City at this particular point in time. The city, across every generation, had been through several waves of turmoil. Our eldest leaders had lived through the Great Depression. Baby boomers like me came of age during the state's economic catastrophe of the 1980s—when it seemed like every year the economy got worse and worse. In the 1990s our youngest residents and professionals had been promised hope with the idea that United Airlines would build its new maintenance facility and bring thousands of good-paying jobs. But again and again, our hopes were dashed.

Marty Grubbs's Prophetic Message

The citizens were then offered hope with the passage of the 1993 MAPS initiative, but at this point, over a year later, MAPS had produced nothing except some early controversy. It was over budget. It was behind schedule. The leaders were pointing fingers at each other. I think at that moment, if there could have been another vote on MAPS, the citizens would have voted it down. And now, here we were in the spring of 1995.

So, consider these unique groups of people that made up Oklahoma City. And imagine the tremendous weight on their collective shoulders: the emotional burden of one of the largest mass murders in American history.

The first Sunday after the bombing, when most of us were still in shock and denial, I listened as my church pastor, Marty Grubbs, tried to add perspective and optimism.

After saying all the predictable, obligatory things about the struggles we were enduring, he closed with a sentence that I never forgot. "I know it seems difficult to imagine right now," he began. "But somehow, I believe something positive is going to come out of all of this."

I like Marty. And I almost always felt better after listening to his Sunday sermons. But this time, I thought he had lost his mind. He seemed to be in denial. His words seemed absurdly optimistic. Something positive was going to come out of this?

There were still over one hundred people buried beneath the rubble downtown! We were living in a daze. The funerals were just beginning and whether we attended or not, we felt the loss of each and every one of those people. They were our relatives, our friends, and our neighbors. We were waking up every day, putting one foot in front of the other and reminding ourselves that the bombing had really happened. It wasn't a nightmare. It was real. And something positive was going to come of this?

Weird thing is, he nailed it. Now with over twenty years of hindsight, I realize that Pastor Marty Grubbs was right.

In the months and years following the bombing, it was as if the citizens of Oklahoma City collectively grabbed hands, pulled each other up, and dared the world to pull us apart. We had been through too much—and, importantly, *we had been through it together.*

Just as two people who go through an emotional experience can emerge with a special bond that no one else can really understand or totally appreciate, so can an entire community share transformative ordeals. After the bombing, Oklahoma City residents grieved and mourned and ultimately healed together.

About two years later, in 1998, having emerged from the economic and emotional turmoil, we were once again ready for great things. We were once again starting to feel optimistic. And we were once again ready for the investments we had made in our community to pay off.

Conservative Principles Driving Civic Investment

On April 16, 1998, the first of the nine MAPS projects opened. More than fourteen thousand people celebrated opening day with the Oklahoma City RedHawks, our AAA baseball team, in the team's new stadium. It was built on the edge of downtown in an area called Bricktown that had long been forgotten. Less than a mile from the central business district, Bricktown was a pretty rough tract of land on what was once the wrong side of the railroad tracks. Filled with warehouses in the 1930s and 1940s, it had become a ghost town by the 1980s. The brick buildings and brick streets in this neighborhood were empty and falling into disrepair.

With the MAPS vote, citizens said yes to revitalizing this neighborhood. Because of the one-cent sales tax, we were able to build a state-of-the-art $34 million stadium in the traditional style, as Camden Yards in Baltimore had re-created just a few years earlier. This was a great ballpark that was warm and friendly, a nostalgic place. It was much better than the voters who had approved MAPS more than four years earlier could have envisioned. And the euphoria surrounding the opening was not only genuine, it was also the turning point for the damaged psyche of Oklahoma City. This was the day that a huge wave of emotional pride emerged and swept over the masses for the first time in at least a generation. This ballpark was worth showing off to visitors. This ballpark was worth inviting family and friends from other parts of the country to come and experience. At least it seemed that way. And amazingly, this was only the *first* MAPS project. There were still eight more to come.

On opening night, two mayors threw out a ceremonial opening pitch and symbolically, but not officially, handed off the leadership of the city. Mayor Norick had finished his third and final term two days before the season opener. His successor was another businessman, Kirk Humphreys. Mayor Norick is now retired. He is considered the father of MAPS and a genuine Oklahoma City hero. And yet, he left office before the projects were completed.

Stop to appreciate an important aspect of the Oklahoma City story: Although Norick had used his political capital to pass the MAPS initiative, it was still at this point a work in progress. As Norick was leaving office, only one of the projects was officially completed. It was Norick who had painstakingly compiled the list of projects and rallied the dissenting interest groups to work together to pass the initiative. It was he who'd had to face the city hall news media time and time again to explain why a project was behind schedule or over budget. But it would be his successor that would oversee the considerable remaining construction and cut the ribbons. This clean hand-off from one mayor to the next was fairly unique. Nevertheless, it is now the model and expectation in Oklahoma City.

In most cities, especially cities with strong mayor models of government, most of the top lieutenants go when a new mayor takes office. For city hall staffers who were loyal to the last leader, they don't want to work for the new kid on the block. And chances are, the new mayor doesn't want them, either. But in Oklahoma City most people stay. When I was elected mayor after three years on city council, my office moved from one end of the hallway to the other. And I was the only one who changed offices. The entire staff remained in place in their offices and their jobs.

Over my service as mayor, one of the most common questions I was asked by outsiders who study MAPS and its funding was "In one of the most conservative political climates in the country, how has Oklahoma City continually passed tax initiatives?"

The best answer I could give went something like this: The

citizens in our very conservative voting pool seem to have determined the type of tax they are willing to consider. There are taxes they like and taxes they don't like.

First, we seem to like capital projects. MAPS is always about building something. When it's done, you can go up and touch it. It may be a building or a stadium or a bike trail, but it's not a program. Voters in Oklahoma City are leery of funding social programs that don't seem to be efficiently run and have mixed results at best.

Second, MAPS is a sales tax. People in Oklahoma City don't like paying property taxes. Perhaps it has something to do with that original Land Run giveaway in 1889. Land has always been cheap in Oklahoma, and low property taxes are part of that concept. Property taxes are placed upon you by government, while sales taxes seem much more discretionary. Plus, about a third of the sales tax in Oklahoma City is paid by people who live outside the city limits. Who doesn't like other people paying their taxes for them?

Third, MAPS programs are authorized for a specific length of time. The voters know how long the tax will be in effect. And they know that when it expires, they will have the opportunity to consider a new plan, or perhaps to end the tax entirely. The voters are in control.

Fourth, MAPS involves the citizenry in the oversight of the construction. To be clear, the citizen oversight has evolved over the years and each of the three iterations of MAPS has played out slightly differently, but the voters know that not all of the decisions will be dictated by one elected official, or a city bureaucrat, or some overpaid consultant. The citizens are directly involved in the process. They get to weigh in every time an architect or engineer is hired. They get to offer an opinion on every meaningful decision in the process.

Sometimes, this slows things down. If we need one of our citizens' advisory boards to decide something and the members have a question, it can delay the discussion for a month until they meet again. But our staff has learned through the process. If staff members think a decision might be contentious or there is a time limit, they plan for that. In the end, the elected officials have the final say, but over 99 percent of the time the citizen oversight committee's vote is in agreement with the final decision.

In today's political climate, transparency is a must—and MAPS is a model of citizen oversight and involvement. If voters feel like they aren't in charge of their government's direction, they can sometimes act out irrationally to prove a point. Let me give you an example.

Back in 2004, an Oklahoma City suburban school district named Mustang was planning a December ballot for a bond issue. The district was growing quickly and needed the funds to build a new grade school. Bond issues in Oklahoma require 60 percent voter approval, so they are not always the easiest elections to win. However, the patrons in this district had a long history of supporting their schools. Mustang had passed every school bond issue as far back as anyone could remember, and there was no reason to think it would be different this time. But this time it *would* be different. This time the school bond issue would fail.

The week before the vote, the superintendent announced that schools would no longer be able to include a Nativity scene in their annual Christmas program. Several parents were upset. They encouraged a state senator to get involved and, before you know it, there was an active telephone campaign to vote against the bond issue.

Now, the point of this story is not to weigh the merits of

having a Nativity scene in a public school. The point is that because the voters did not get to vote on the exclusion of the Nativity scene, they expressed their anger the only way they knew how. They sent a message to administrators by voting against the bond issue.

This kind of thing often happens in communities across America. Voters don't have a direct say on taxation votes in Washington and they also don't have a direct say on almost all of the taxation votes in their state capitals. So, because the taxes that voters do have a direct say over are almost exclusively local taxes, those get extra scrutiny. Local government officials try to communicate the merits of a local tax initiative and local voters respond with emotional answers like "Don't they get it? We are taxed enough!" Many vote no in local elections simply because they are mad at their state and national governments.

People tend to vote for different candidates and different initiatives for different reasons, but I believe that most people vote as the result of an emotion as opposed to the result of an intellectual process. That's why so many voters can't be convinced with facts. When you are tied to an emotion, facts are not important. And if you feel like your state and national governments are wasting your tax dollars, it may not matter that your local government actually has a well-constructed, well-meaning initiative that deserves consideration.

And there is one more aspect of the MAPS initiatives that deserves pointing out. In most cities, when a capital project is approved by a vote of the people, the elected leaders then borrow the money to build the project and use future tax revenue to pay off the debt. This is a *bonding* method and it is used in almost all situations.

With these MAPS initiatives, there was no bonding. There was no debt. We simply collected the sales tax, and paid cash for each expense along the way. This created a multitude of opportunities and challenges.

But the major challenge was that it took longer to build the projects. Paying cash is great, but you have to wait until the tax dollars accumulate. This can take years and years and has political consequences. An elected official who uses his political capital to pass an initiative usually wants the project built as soon as possible to help create support for his reelection. But not in Oklahoma City. Remember, it was Ron Norick's successor, Kirk Humphreys, who assumed oversight for completing the projects.

In many political transitions, a new mayor means new ideas and new projects. Many times, a new mayor will stop a previous effort if possible. In fact, they may have even run for office pledging to stop a project. If Humphreys had not accepted the huge responsibilities of his predecessor, MAPS likely would not have been completed and developed into the success story it has become. In Oklahoma City, it is now the norm for mayors to fulfill the vision of their predecessors and add their own ideas along the way.

Building Schools? Or Paving the Streets with Gold?

Humphreys took office just as MAPS was becoming a reality. Although public opinion was swinging city hall's way, many of the projects were struggling individually. For example, some of the projects expanded to include parking structures that hadn't been considered originally. And of course each of the projects was built by the lowest competitive bidder. So, oversight of the projects meant dealing with contractors who were trying to squeeze out a profit for themselves. It wasn't always easy. Humphreys and the city council had their hands full.

There was also another large issue that was a growing concern: education.

Like many American cities, the urban core of Oklahoma City had witnessed a mass exodus of residents in the 1970s and 1980s. The tipping point occurred when a federal judge imposed integration in the Oklahoma City Public Schools in the early '70s. Half of all families left the school district within two decades.

But while some families relocated to neighboring suburbs, which was the case for many other municipalities across the country, Oklahoma City had such a large footprint that many families relocated to different school districts, while still living within the city limits. This was one of the realities that made the original MAPS work: The city could invest in its downtown while taxing its more affluent citizens who were living in the suburbs. In MAPS, the tax dollars we collected were spent many miles away from neighborhoods on the outer rings of town. We were able to convince them that the quality of life downtown had a direct impact on the suburbs.

MAPS had given Oklahoma City a boost in culture and nightlife in the downtown, but while people were now going downtown to watch a ballgame in the new stadium, they were still living in the suburbs. It was at this point that Mayor Humphreys wondered why people were coming downtown to have fun but nobody was moving there.

A city staffer finally made the comment: "Mayor, we could pave the streets of downtown with gold. But if the schools don't improve, no one is going to call downtown home."

To an outsider—and even a few insiders—Oklahoma City

schools are a confusing mix of districts. Within the city boundaries, there are twenty-four separate school districts, each with its own elected school board and budget. Some of the districts are K through 6. Some are K through 12. And only one of them is called the Oklahoma City Public School System. This district, which served the city center, had 40 percent of the city's kids. And it was in trouble.

Like most urban districts, Oklahoma City was facing all sorts of overwhelming social issues *outside* the classroom that seemed to keep educators from having success *inside* the classroom. In addition, the district was full of inefficiencies. Through the years, the district enrollment had shrunk nearly by half but the geographic footprint of the district had not changed. So, the schools had half as many kids and half as much funding. And yet the transportation needs were the same, so you had half-full buses going to half-full schools over a geographic area that was twice as large as it needed to be.

Poverty rates were high. Parental involvement was low. More and more kids were not speaking English. Teachers were overwhelmed.

By state law, an elected school board was supposed to be making the tough decisions necessary to keep the district on track. But over time it was easy to see that the school board had lost the support of the voters. The district could no longer pass its bond issues. The deferred maintenance was piling up. Someone did the math and determined that even if the district did start passing its local bond issues, the pre-existing condition of the schools meant that they would never catch up to the deferred maintenance issues that already existed.

As the city tried to use the story of MAPS to lure businesses, it was easy to see that economic development was tied to the success of the local schools. MAPS or no MAPS,

Oklahoma City was not going to be a significant job creator if it could not improve the image of its schools.

In many cities, mayors have a lot of control over their local schools. In fact, in some urban centers like New York and Chicago, cities and their mayors run the schools. This was not the case in Oklahoma City. In fact, the role of mayor did not include any aspect of operating the local schools because the city didn't fund their operating budgets and was not involved in new school construction. The city was not involved in the school bus system, and the city's police department was not responsible for securing the safety of the kids. I suppose if a school caught on fire, it was the city's fire department that was expected to extinguish the blaze, but that's about it.

There was also a disconnect between the urban school district and the business community. The vast majority of business leaders lived far from the city center in suburbia. Their kids were attending private schools or public school in one of the other twenty-three districts that served kids that lived inside the Oklahoma City limits.

The fact that there were so many different school districts serving our kids was part of the problem. But the biggest problem facing the Oklahoma City school district was the disconnect between the leadership of the community and the district itself. It seemed like no one wanted to take ownership of the problem.

The paradigm shift began when the business community and Mayor Humphreys (and, of course, Humphreys was from the business community) decided that the school system's plight had become a civic emergency and could no longer be ignored. Despite MAPS, Oklahoma City was not going to have success in economic development as long as its largest school district was floundering.

So now what? Now that they had identified a civic issue and generated the will to address it, where to start?

Here's a retrospective look at the steps that we took to ensure some accountability:

1. Take some ownership of the political process that decides who serves on the school board. Find good candidates and support them.
2. Make sure all elected officials in the community understand the importance of the issue. Too often, city councils and county officials worry only about their own silos and direct sphere of influence. All political leaders needed to understand that the struggles of the school district were everyone's problem.
3. Get the business community on board and get the media on board. Perhaps we often think of these two as adversaries, but there's no reason to avoid asking for help from each of those groups when the future of your city is at stake.

As the chamber of commerce and Mayor Humphreys worked to enlighten the leadership of the community, they all became more aware of the difficulties they would face going forward. If the city was going to use a MAPS approach to try and help the district, they would need to change state law.

By law, the overhead of education—which is to say, teacher salaries and other expenses—was funded by the state. Local school districts hired administrators to oversee the operations of their schools and needed voter approval for school construction. There was to be no involvement from cities. School districts had their own geographic boundaries and their own elected leaders. Basically, cities and mayors were supposed to mind their own business and leave the schools alone.

In the year 2000, Humphreys was two years into his first term. Even though the MAPS projects were still being constructed, the MAPS tax had ended and the sales tax had reverted to its previous level. He approached the governor and state legislative leaders about changing state law so that Oklahoma City could become the financial savior of the state's largest school system.

The legislation that passed created two new concepts. First, a large city could hold an election to fund capital projects for its schools. Second, a new at-large school board position would be created. It was designed to mirror the governance structure that had worked well in city councils for decades. The new position would be called the chairman of the school board but would in essence serve like a mayor and give the district a political identity. In other words, just like cities had a mayor elected by the entire city electorate and a city council elected by wards, the school board would have a chairman elected at-large and a school board elected by individual districts.

One of our most distinguished business leaders, Cliff Hudson, the CEO of Sonic restaurants, agreed to run for the new position—which was, in and of itself, very promising. Hudson was well respected in the business community. He had an impressive skill set and obviously wasn't running for school board for personal gain. By taking the job and making the commitment to help our city's schools, he lent his credibility to the school board and raised its profile among all citizens.

Humphreys then worked to put together a funding concept that he hoped the community as a whole would support. Basically, the entire city would once again be asked to increase its sales tax rate by a penny for seven years. The money would be spent on schools but would not be spent proportionally. Seventy percent of the money would go to capital projects inside the Oklahoma City school district. The remaining 30 percent would be distributed to the twenty-three remaining districts that served kids living inside the city limits.

The money would be collected by the city. All of the project construction that took place in the Oklahoma City district would be administered by the city and overseen by a new city trust that Humphreys established. If all this sounds complicated, trust me, it was much more complicated than I described.

The initiative would be called MAPS for Kids.

The Hall of Fame for Political Vision

As MAPS for Kids was being created and presented to voters in 2001, I was just getting started in my career on the city council. I was proud to help with the project, but I was really impressed with the level of effort and political skills my new colleagues put to work.

I watched as Humphreys and the other leaders convinced all twenty-four school boards to support the plan. Do you know how hard it is to convince one school board to support some never-before-tried-anywhere concept? Try convincing twenty-four. It's especially hard when one of the districts would get the lion's share of the revenues—70 percent—and the other twenty-three would divide 30 percent. Part of Humphreys's argument to the outlying districts was something like, "Look, if you say no, you get zero. If you say yes, you at least get a share of the pot."

If there is ever a hall of fame built for politics, MAPS for

Kids should be inducted for incredible achievements in consensus building. Despite the obvious headwinds, and plenty of ways the proposal could have faltered, MAPS for Kids passed with 62 percent of the vote.

Humphreys and Hudson and the other business leaders who got involved deserve a world of credit for getting it done. But I would also add that this was in that golden era of civic pride in Oklahoma City. This was *after the bombing* and *as the MAPS projects were opening.*

The city had political capital to spare and loaned it to the school district to provide a massive new round of capital projects. All seventy-five buildings in the district were rebuilt new or refurbished. That construction included a new round of digital technology. An entire new fleet of school buses was purchased.

The benefits went beyond education. From an economic development standpoint, MAPS for Kids made investments in seventy-five neighborhoods that very few others were investing in. The city government was coming in and investing millions in neighborhood schools, and neighbors became more likely to invest in their own homes. Even if it was something small like fixing the porch or adding some landscaping, it helped the neighborhood in immeasurable ways.

And then, with a new school and well-cared-for homes, the neighborhood becomes a more appealing place for a small businessperson to open a sandwich shop or a gift store. MAPS for Kids began focused solely on education but it came to affect so much more.

You can certainly argue that constructing new buildings doesn't necessarily change the education going on inside the building. That's true. It's now over fifteen years later and the district continues to be a work in progress. But in a post–MAPS for Kids Oklahoma City, one very important component contin-ues: The leadership and the community now embrace the dis-trict's challenges as everyone's challenges. There is no longer a disconnect between the city and the business community and the schools. The paradigm shift that began with MAPS for Kids continues.

ALBUQUERQUE: A BETTER WAY TO FIGHT POVERTY AND HOMELESSNESS

I'm a card-carrying Republican, so one of the key takeaways from the stories of MAPS and MAPS for Kids is that the government, in its best role, focuses on doing the kind of work that encourages private employment and investment, and homes in on programs and projects that operate well at scale.

Usually, complicated social issues like poverty, inequality, healthcare, and addiction are just too nuanced and dependent on individualized attention and compassionate care for government bureaucracies to deal with them well. There *is* a role for government, but legislation is a blunt tool for dealing with real people caught in dire circumstances. And for those of us serious about finally breaking through the noise and making progress fighting poverty, addiction, and human suffering, a serious effort to strengthen the best institutions for the job is badly needed.

Over the past few years in Albuquerque, New Mexico, I've seen one of the best examples of conservative principles driving social change making a real impact. Under the leadership of then mayor Richard Berry the city began addressing homelessness, which disproportionately affects veterans and people who are suffering from layers of depression, addiction, and mental illness. And what's amazing about the story is how easy it was for him to get started.

Let's rewind for a second. Richard Berry was elected mayor of Albuquerque in 2009, the first Republican to take that office in two and a half decades. In the region, Democrats outnumber Republicans by at least 50 percent. As a city, Albuquerque has a deep sense of its Native American heritage, its rich connections to Mexico, and a certain spirituality among the people that might scare off a buttoned-up conservative like me from taking the plunge to run for a job in city hall. How the heck did he beat the incumbent Democrat by almost ten points? I wanted to know, so I asked him.

"Pretty simple. I asked for the job," Mayor Berry explains. Voters still like integrity and results above party loyalty. And evidently, they believed he earnestly wanted the work.

A few years later, an echo of Mayor Berry's line is unfolding in Albuquerque, where the city government took the lead by providing people with an honest day's work, a little bit of income, and a realistic first step toward making their lives measurably better. Like a lot of the best ideas, the beauty is in just how simple it actually is.

We have all at some point seen people standing on a street corner or an interstate on-ramp with a simple cardboard sign saying WILL WORK FOR FOOD. Many of us have reached into our pockets or purse in response, found an extra dollar or some loose change, and rolled down our window. We all know instinctively this isn't the ideal way to lend a helping hand. But most of us have done it with the belief in the back of our minds that the recipient is interested in more than a meal. With the right support, they earnestly seek a pathway out of their current circumstance.

Sadly, political arguments on hunger, poverty, and addiction get more caught up in ideology than practicality—and our neighbors in need are far too often caught out in the cold. But in an insight that's really only news to lifetime politicians and partisan hacks, there's a better way—for both parties—to make real progress. At the heart of Mayor Berry's idea, shared in his 2017 TED Talk, is this note: "We know people are more likely to invest in themselves if the community is willing to invest in them first."

The program Mayor Berry started is called "There's a Better Way," and here's how it works: City hall has an endless demand for work to get done, be it trash pickup, lot cleanup, or graffiti cover-up. Albuquerque has organizations that are built to work with people at the most personal, emotional, and spiritual levels. And like any place, the city has more people in dire circumstances than the traditionally structured, centrally run government organizations can serve.

Many of those people whom government services *don't* reach end up on Albuquerque street corners and on-ramps—and A Better Way begins its work by meeting people where they are. The city government fixed up an extra passenger van in its fleet and handed the keys over to a local non-profit that goes to where people are standing on corners panhandling.

Instead of offering some loose change that may not be used for food, but rather to feed an addiction, they are offered a decent wage for a day's work, a healthy meal, and a chance to contribute to a project that will make the city better. In keeping with the long-term mission of the project, each worker is offered services and counseling through one of the city's non-profit initiatives that fight homelessness and addiction.

By early 2017, when Mayor Berry gave his terrific TED Talk, they had cleaned up hundreds of vacant lots, offered thousands of hours of work, and connected over two hundred workers to permanent, full-time jobs. Among veterans, the U.S. Department of Housing and Urban Development had declared that the city had reduced its official veterans' homelessness rate to functional zero. Through A Better Way and other homelessness initiatives during Mayor Berry's time in office, Albuquerque lowered unsheltered homelessness by 80 percent and chronic homelessness by at least 40 percent.

Essential to the program's success is the practice of relying on non-profits and churches with the ability and willingness to treat people with individual attention and the particular grace and dignity they deserve.

If the city were hiring the workers directly, the mountain of paperwork per individual would take two weeks or even two months to get through, not a couple of hours. As Berry jokes, imagine pulling up next to a panhandler or a homeless person, offering them a job, and telling them you'll be back to pick them up in six weeks.

One other important point about what makes it "A Better Way." Government provides the basics—the infrastructure (the van) and the core funding (in this case about $50,000 for the entire first year), while non-profits and service and faith groups work with people in need. Each party does what it is best at. For a relatively modest investment of infrastructure and capital, Albuquerque has provided thousands of hours of service to the city and offered hundreds of people and families a credible, productive alternative to the choices they faced previously.

The simplicity of the approach, the role of government providing the basic infrastructure, working with private partners and non-profits to focus on what they do best is also key to another marker of Mayor Berry's insight—how easy it is to scale and replicate. Across Albuquerque, to be sure—but across the country and around the globe as well. Just a year after launching in Albuquerque, several other cities in the United States and around the world reached out to Berry to pick up where he started. And the only reason we didn't follow suit in Oklahoma City was that the leaders in my community had so many great projects under way already. But the key insights of working with the right partners at the right time is a lesson we should all continue to work with, no matter where we are starting.

A mistake we often make when working through government to solve social problems is focusing on what government can prohibit or require people to do. Passing laws or ordinances that set community standards is sometimes a good idea, but as Mayor Berry puts it, "You can outlaw the act, but you can't outlaw the struggles that people face." Sometimes we have to think about what government can *encourage*, or the kinds of actions government's leadership can *incentivize* or *accelerate*. Maybe this is just something that mayors know instinctively. We can't really hide behind laws or blame our political parties for inaction. For us, the people our work affects are only an arm's length away.

But just as often, my colleagues in the Republican Party are criticized for being uncaring to people in need and unconcerned about the lives of people we don't understand. I think that's a pretty bad rap. Despite what you've heard, conservatives *do* care about improving the lives of people in need. The principles that guide our thinking may be different from those on the other side of the aisle, but most of the time the end goal is the same.

And when that goal is clear, when different players focus on what they are best at, and when government dollars are used in the best way, we can make the most progress to build stronger families and communities.

CHAPTER 4

From Mow to Row

By the year 2000, several of the big MAPS development projects were under way. The voters of Oklahoma City could see that the promise of putting water in the river was going to be a reality. The first of three low-water dams was under construction. And while the river was still dry, there was talk that the construction of the dams might lead to some water-front development someday.

One day about that time, a young lawyer named Mike Knopp drove in from the suburbs to downtown Oklahoma City and got out of his car. He stood along the edge of this big waterless ditch that traversed the heart of his hometown and started to see potential. Potential for something that probably not one other person in Oklahoma could see.

Technically, he was standing on the bank of the North Canadian River. But doesn't a river have water? There wasn't a drop in sight. It must have been the worst excuse for a river in the world. How bad was it? Oklahoma City had a line item in its budget to actually *mow* "the river" twice a year.

Looking down at his feet, Mike could see an ugly mixture of weeds and sand, empty pop cans and trash. Along the bank, there were thousands of large rocks and surplus concrete just dumped there by government engineers and downtown developers decades before. More than anything, our river was a garbage heap.

But somehow, and I'm still not sure how, Mike looked past the eyesore and saw the future.

Ignored or Despised:
The Ditch the Grown-Ups Called a River

The Canadian River, which starts in Colorado and flows through New Mexico, Texas, and Oklahoma, had been winding its way through the Great Plains for thousands of years. Historians noted how frequently it changed course, chewing up the sandy soil and becoming a moving target for mapmakers of the past.

Oklahoma City was founded in 1889 on the spot where the river met the railroad. The earliest Sooners understood the importance of water and built their lives around it to the extent they needed to. But it was always seen as a means to an end, I guess. For most of that first century, depending on how the river behaved, Oklahomans had mostly either ignored or despised it.

What good was it? It was never really navigable so it wasn't much good for trade. And from time to time in the early twentieth century it flooded and created enormous problems downtown. The river flooded twice in 1923, and the idea of a city with a riverfront stopped adding up. There's one local legend about an entrepreneur who had built a hotel along the riverfront just a few years earlier. After one of the floods that year, the river actually moved a few hundred yards away, *overnight*.

The city leadership had finally had enough. They began the

process of convincing the federal government that something needed to be done. A couple of decades later, a dam was built ninety miles upstream and the flooding issues were addressed for good. For those first few generations, Oklahomans had fought the river. In the 1940s, they finally killed it.

When I was growing up, I remember how our schoolbooks showed pictures of the Mississippi or the Thames or the Seine—or even the Nile and the Amazon. And how our teachers told us about the power that rivers have in shaping history. But for us, there was only a ditch downtown that the grownups called a river.

But it was not only an annoyance and an eyesore. Geographically and emotionally, it split Oklahoma City in two.

The neighborhoods to the south were largely working class and slowly developed a blue-collar sense of pride. It was not unusual to hear someone say they were "proud to be from south Oklahoma City." But after a while, it began to sound a little bit defensive, as if "southsiders" had to convince themselves or someone else of their worth.

I never heard anyone say they were "proud to be from *north* Oklahoma City," which was more white collar and had expanded rapidly with the suburban flight of the 1950s and 1960s. To my knowledge, people in the affluent sections of far north Oklahoma City didn't think less of southsiders—they simply didn't think about the river at all! But the division it created was wide, and the tension it created was something we started to understand only after the barrier had been removed.

In the early 1990s, after the impact of generations of neglect became clear, the idea of putting water in the river had become a broad civic priority. Tulsa, our sister city, had a real river, the Arkansas—yet all we had was this scar in the earth that had been an embarrassment for long enough.

When the soon-to-be-transformational MAPS initiative was created in 1993, the river was a focal point of the campaign. The idea was to build three low-water dams southwest of downtown and impound the water from occasional upstream rains that had never before been captured. Putting water in the river was now politically popular.

But the MAPS improvements promised little beyond the hard infrastructure. It was difficult to imagine that the river would be a catalyst for much. Would we be able to fish in it? Of course. But we already had plenty of good fishing lakes in central Oklahoma. Could we put a boat in it? Oh, sure, the city planned to construct a place to launch small boats. But there wasn't any place to go except right back to the boat ramp. And from the water there sure wasn't much to see.

Around the world, riverfront property is highly valued and riverfront development creates economic development. But that wasn't the case here. Not then. Because the river had been such an eyesore, there was no significant development along its banks, and to be honest, we couldn't imagine that there would be. We just wanted water to cosmetically improve the landscape and perhaps ease the embarrassment. Anything positive beyond that would be a bonus.

As Mike Knopp stood along the top of the ugly, rocky bank, the first dam was under construction and the next two were still being designed. Water was a promise yet to be delivered. The desert of sand, trash, and weeds was still an overwhelming eyesore.

Mike tried to visualize what the future would hold. Only *he* seemed to grasp the opportunity. After the course of the riverbed twisted south and then back north across the southern edge of downtown, it straightened out for almost a half mile. It wasn't just *kind* of straight, it was *perfectly* straight. The

engineers that had dealt with the flooding problems a generation before had redirected the path of the river and made that
section a straight line. Mike believed they had accidentally engineered an opportunity to create the finest venue in the world
for the sports of canoe, rowing, and kayak.

What's a Kayak, Anyway?

At that time in football-crazy Oklahoma, I am not sure many
even knew that canoeing, rowing, and kayaking were competitive sports. Canoes were something we saw in historical depic-
tions of Native Americans. Rowing was what you did if the
outboard motor on your bass boat conked out. And a kayak?
I'm not positive I could have spelled the word on my first try.

Mike was unique. Although he'd grown up in suburban
Oklahoma City, he'd been introduced to rowing in the 1980s
while attending Oklahoma State University in Stillwater. On a
rural lake, ten miles from much of anything, some OSU students had started a rowing club.

Mike remembers that club was rowing in its most rudimentary form. When he tells the story to new rowers, he smiles as
he remembers the OSU boats that might have sunk at any moment. The paddles and other rowing equipment were old and
had been discarded by actual rowing programs in other states.
It was less of a sport than a chance to soak up the sunshine,
get some exercise, and drink a few beers. Rowing in rural Oklahoma provided it all.

Eventually, his college buddies moved on, but Mike went to
law school about eighty miles south in Norman and brought his
hobby with him. He put together a new group of friends who
rowed in pre-dawn anonymity on one of the city's lakes. Anyone

who happened to see them really might have been startled. What business would anyone have on a boat in the middle of the lake before dawn? Surely they were up to no good!

And with a handful of ex-astronauts living in our state, there were probably more citizens that had been in outer space than had been in a real live rowing competition. But even this fact didn't seem to deter Mike.

To paraphrase Victor Hugo: *Nothing is as powerful as an idea whose time has come.* Mike sensed the opportunity. The river in Oklahoma City had the potential not just to succeed, but to become a truly world-class rowing venue.

First of all, the new river would not have a current and that could be an advantage in attracting competitions. The new "river" would really just be a series of three lakes. Water would be impounded. So the vast majority of the time, there would be no flow at all. Secondly, the water line was ten to twenty feet below the surrounding terrain. That would limit the amount of wind that would affect a competition. And that straightaway! That man-made, geometrically perfect stretch of river would be ideal for racing. It was like a drag strip! Mike couldn't think of an existing river rowing course anywhere in the world that had that going for it.

So, now what? The first problem was financial. He didn't really have any money to put into the project. So Mike started talking to people and landed an opportunity to speak to Oklahoma City's downtown Rotary Club. With several hundred attending weekly, it is one of the largest Rotary gatherings in the world. He gave the crowd a description of his idea. He tried to paint a picture for them but the feedback on the presentation was mixed. He was a nice enough guy. He had completed law school, so he obviously wasn't stupid. But this idea of his was still borderline crazy.

Undeterred, Mike continued his quest and talked to some local non-profit foundations. The leaders listened politely and then agreed with the Rotary Club: The idea seemed a little farfetched.

By 2004, though, there was actually water in the river. The three MAPS-approved dams were phased in with the final one completed that year. Getting a boat into the water was still tricky, but at least now Mike had an opportunity to help people see his overall vision. He made sure he was taking boats on the water almost immediately following the construction of the dams and kept talking up his vision for a rowing facility.

Mike wasn't a flamboyant salesman who would stage a press conference to announce his dream. Nor was he even a downtown guy or a city leader. He was just a lawyer who lived in the suburbs and made his way downtown every day. So it became his habit to casually mention his ideas to leaders in the community, trying to plant the seed for what he knew could grow into something big.

Eventually, he landed a meeting with the organizers of the Sooner State Games, which is kind of an athletic smorgasbord that attracts hundreds of amateur competitors in different sports to gather for a weekend to compete. The event was first held in the 1980s and the list of sports included in the competitions changed every year. The organizers allowed Mike to hold a rowing competition so people could see boats in the water.

Still, even though rowing fit into the games, it didn't feel like the start of anything lasting. I'm sure if you'd asked people about it, they'd have said it wouldn't happen again.

A Jolt of Energy for Rowing in the River

It probably wouldn't have lasted more than an afternoon if not for a corporate team from one of our state's most important companies: Chesapeake Energy. Chesapeake's founder and CEO, Aubrey McClendon, had encouraged his leadership team to be active in the community for years. As part of that effort, the company sent a bunch of beginning rowers to the Sooner State Games, including a company executive named Martha Burger, who still sits on the OKC Boathouse Foundation board after her retirement from Chesapeake.

McClendon also told his executive team to let him know if they met anyone with good ideas. McClendon had grown up in Oklahoma City and was a history major at Duke University. He had a curious intellect. He loved his hometown. If people had ideas that could improve the community, he wanted to meet them. Burger told McClendon about Mike and his hope of building a small boathouse.

Because McClendon had grown up in Oklahoma City, at first he joined the chorus of people who thought the idea of rowing in the North Canadian River was kind of crazy. But McClendon was an oil and gas maverick with a reputation as a risk-taker. And because he had been to Duke, he had witnessed and understood the rowing culture.

Mike was surprised when McClendon actually showed up that Saturday to watch his company's team compete in the Sooner State Games. Since there was only a handful of specta- tors along the rocky bank, Mike was able to spot McClendon standing near the put-in, so he walked over to thank him for attending the incredibly rudimentary event.

Somehow McClendon was impressed. Maybe it was the way

Mike treated the competitors. Maybe it was the enthusiasm that the rowers displayed for their sport. Maybe it was Mike's passion. But something McClendon saw sparked an interest.

A few days after the games, McClendon and Burger invited Mike to a meeting at the corporate headquarters. The Chesapeake campus in Oklahoma City is like none other in the energy industry. Unlike the skyscrapers of steel and glass in Dallas and Houston, Chesapeake HQ is a heavily landscaped series of buildings in a Georgian architectural style designed by Oklahoma's noted architect Rand Elliott, who joined in the meeting.

"Mike," McClendon began, "I get it. I see now what you are trying to do."

I'm not even sure *Mike* knew what Mike was trying to do. But McClendon was a visionary. Exactly the kind of ally a guy like Knopp needed.

Knopp had been trying to raise about $300,000, which he figured would allow him to build some kind of metal structure to store boats and keep the rowing community alive. To Mike and his small but growing group of rowing enthusiasts, that would be incredible. That would be enough. They would no longer have to carry their boats from the team's garage blocks away to the river every time they wanted to practice.

But how much would McClendon be willing to donate? Could Mike make some real progress toward his fund-raising goal? With a meaningful donation from Chesapeake blessing his work, could he be on the road to building his dream?

Mike had brought along some drawings of the building that he wanted to construct. In retrospect, it looked more like a fishing shack than anything else. He knew $300,000 was a lot of money but he made the ask.

McClendon was kind and careful to not totally dismiss

Mike's vision. But Mike could tell McClendon had something else on his mind.

"Mike, if we are going to do this, let's do it right." Then he turned to the architect. "Rand, have you ever designed a boat-house?"

Elliott had won several international architectural awards for a variety of projects but this was new territory. "No, I haven't," he said.

"Do you think you *could* design a boathouse?" McClendon asked. "A really good one?"

"Oh yeah," Elliott replied, quickly realizing the opportunity placed in front of him. "I think I could design a *really* good boathouse."

From that conversation and Chesapeake's initial support sprang a truly incredible series of private-sector investments along the river. The plans and schematics for the modest build-ing Mike was hoping to build were basically tossed into the wastebasket. The price tag on Elliott's boathouse, which McClendon largely funded, wound up being $3.5 million.

When it opened in 2006, the international rowing commu-nity took notice. The Chesapeake Boathouse, as it was chris-tened, looks like Noah's Ark. Its curved roofline and twenty-four-foot-tall wall of glass has space for 124 rowing shells, a fully equipped training facility, and a meeting space. An iconic structure on the north banks of the river, the Ches-apeake Boathouse still draws attention from motorists passing on the nearby Interstate 35 bridge.

Rowing and kayak magazines featured the boathouse in their pages. And Mike and his rowing buddies moved their boats in almost immediately. At the time, the construction of the Chesapeake Boathouse seemed like the beginning and end of Oklahoma City's investment in the sport. It was hard to imagine how our local river sports community could ever grow into it. Even after it opened, we weren't exactly on the radar screen of any national rowing effort.

But today, it is easy to see that the boathouse was the catalyst for the creation of what would become the finest venue in the world for the sports of canoe, rowing, and kayak. The straightaway, that long half-mile of river that Mike discovered on his visit to the river in the 1990s, is now among the highest-profile stretches of water in the world. McClendon's initial investment spurred other philanthropists to get involved. Devon Energy, another local Fortune 500 company, invested $10 million to design and build a boathouse for Oklahoma City University's rowing team that would also serve as the headquarters for the OKC National High Performance Center.

Other universities in and around Oklahoma City quickly built boathouses for their own rowing teams. Other businesses and philanthropic groups from across the state invested in the river and growing boathouse district. And McClendon himself put more money into the growth along the river. The Chesapeake Finish Line Tower, complete with corporate suites, allows hundreds of people to enjoy the annual Oklahoma Regatta Festival. Each October, some five hundred miles from the nearest oceanfront, dozens of the best boating teams and athletes from around the world gather in Oklahoma to compete. Just beneath the surface, now dotted by these boats and the competitors that drive them, used to be a ditch that everyone just ignored.

What was once a picture in Mike's mind has become an interactive rowing, canoe, and kayak mecca with well over $100 million invested. The newer boathouses, all designed by Elliott, are home to the top training facilities in the world. The construction of a man-made whitewater course led USA

Canoe/Kayak to relocate its headquarters from Charlotte to Oklahoma City. Every day, there are world-class athletes training on the only lighted rowing course in the world. The 2012 and 2016 United States Olympic trials were held on what has been renamed the Oklahoma River. Imagine the Olympic trials being held on a stretch of river that had been a ditch just a few years earlier.

Aware that these sports have an upper-crust image, the nonprofit community started inner-city rowing programs to bring the sport to the masses. And that ditch, that eyesore, that used to divide our city in two? It is now a world-class sporting facility that brings people from our little town on the plains together. If all this sounds incredible, it is.

Mike Knopp, Recovering Attorney

Down at the boathouse district, Mike Knopp is still the quiet, driving force. He has put his legal career on pause for the past decade to serve as the executive director of the Boathouse Foundation and continues as a leader with Oklahoma City University's rowing team. McClendon remained actively involved until his death in a car accident in 2016.

So how did all this happen?

In a sense, it is a great example of the power of civic leadership. One after another, individuals stood on the shoulders of those that came before them. In 1993, Oklahoma City leaders convinced the voters to pass MAPS, the initiative that built the dams and put water in the river. Later, Knopp, with his knowledge and enthusiasm for rowing, saw the potential to create a rowing venue. He inspired Burger and McClendon, who funded the vision and encouraged others to get involved.

Government helped out along the way. Oklahoma City responded with more river investment in 2009 with the passage of MAPS 3, another sales tax initiative.

The benefits to Oklahoma City are many. Athletes have relocated from around the world to be near the facilities. Tourism has soared. The river investment continues to add to the quality of life, which in turn continues to attract a lot of highly educated twentysomethings who want to live there. Those types of benefits are quantifiable. With highly educated twentysomethings and a better quality of life, Oklahoma City now attracts corporations looking to build facilities and create jobs.

When Dell Computers was deciding where to locate the company's customer care center, a company executive secretly brought his family to Oklahoma City for a weekend, much as United Airlines executives had years earlier. This time, the Dell execs saw a city changing for the better and wanted to be a part of the story. In my first "job creation" victory as mayor, Dell decided to build a fifty-five-acre site that now houses around two thousand good jobs. At one end of the newly invigorated river lies the boathouse and the Native American Cultural Center. At the other end, a corporate campus built by one of the most innovative, successful brands of the information age.

There is also the improved pride of the community. Ever the historian, McClendon was very aware of the Dust Bowl image of Oklahoma. What could help improve the city's brand more than becoming a modern-day mecca of water sports?

So what have I learned from witnessing all of this? Several things, really. This is a story about finding a hidden asset and unleashing its potential. Most every city has a river. Some cities have two or three. All of these rivers have more potential than Oklahoma City's pitiful North Canadian once had. But potential in hidden assets reaches far beyond rivers and abounds all around us. Beyond rivers, there is hidden potential in parks, lakes, golf courses, old government buildings, and industrial sites.

And most importantly, there are inspirational people like Mike Knopp in these communities that have a vision and are looking for a way to get started. It is true that an unfunded idea is not all that difficult to find. They are everywhere. Sometimes the missing link is the passion of the person with the idea. Take another look at the most recent crazy idea to emerge in your community. Maybe it's not so crazy.

DES MOINES: EMBRACING HISTORY
FOR A RIVERFRONT RENAISSANCE

Just around the time that construction for the whitewater rafting facility was under way in my city, I was invited to Des Moines, Iowa, to give a talk on cities and walkability to the state's Urban Land Institute chapter. I thought I was going to talk about streets and bike lanes—and I did that—but I also learned an important lesson or two about how a smaller city like Des Moines was learning to leverage its waterways and its history in equally creative but very different ways.

On the banks of the Des Moines River, you can see a number of impressive buildings. The city hall, which sits on a street named for Governor Robert D. Ray (who, after twenty years in office at the state capitol, served as mayor of Des Moines), is a building I would love to work in.

Like most state capitals in the country, you can get a little history lesson by reading the street signs and the names of the places and parks as you walk around. On this trip to Des Moines, I learned that one of the world's great opera singers, Simon Estes, was born and raised in Iowa. I learned about the early days of the Conservationist movement and the role Congressman Neal Smith had played in conserving land and wilderness across the state and across our country. But I don't think anything could quite prepare me for the history lesson I received when I got to the place I was invited to give this speech on sidewalks and bike lanes.

I've given a lot of speeches in a lot of pretty underwhelming boardrooms and auditoriums in "modern" buildings that hadn't been modernized in some time. I figured Des Moines would offer a setting along those lines, as I wouldn't put the city on any top-ten list for great architecture. But I was about to get a big surprise.

I love our new riverfront back home, and I love seeing what other cities do with them, too. So I took a little walk to get my steps in for the day on my Fitbit before my speech, as I often do.

All along the banks of the Des Moines River, you could see the marks of progress in recent history. There is a new Riverwalk and a beautiful pedestrian bridge named for Principal Financial, one of the city's biggest private employers. The city hall I mentioned before is quite beautiful, as is the county courthouse—to say nothing of the state capitol building atop a nearby hill, that for diplomatic purposes I will characterize as "just as beautiful as our statehouse in Oklahoma."

Then, I decided to head over to the venue for my speech to the local Urban Land Institute chapter—something called the Norman E. Borlaug World Food Prize Hall of Laureates.

A friend of mine had called to tell me that this venue was pretty special, so I was curious about what I was walking into. I didn't understand the name, but when I arrived, I got it. Essentially, I walked into an architectural and design masterpiece that stands shoulder to shoulder with the most impressive buildings in the world.

Most likely, the building that had been Des Moines's public library since the beginning of the twentieth century was at one point on the verge of being mothballed when the new, high-tech library was finished on the other side of downtown. Instead, what stands there now is a spectacular monument to Iowa's history—and its aspirational future—as a leader in agricultural innovation and humanitarian outreach.

Let me explain what the building is: The World Food Prize is a $250,000 annual award given to scientists, agronomists,

heads of state, and others who have done something spectacular in their careers to "improve the quality, quantity, or availability of food in the world." Think of it as the Nobel Prize in
the fight against hunger.

Walking around this building, I learned about its namesake,
Norman Borlaug. In 1970, he—an agronomist and Iowa
native—won the Nobel Peace Prize for his efforts sparking the
global "Green Revolution" that helped prevent a massive wave
of starvation around the world. Borlaug worked for the Rockefeller Foundation in Mexico in the 1940s, and his scientific
research had a powerful—and staggeringly fast—impact on
agriculture and the fight against hunger.

You see, agricultural scientists had developed some pretty
good ideas for ways to make plants stronger, less susceptible to
disease, able to produce more food. But traditional cross-
breeding would take decades to coax these changes out of our
staple crops. With mass starvation for hundreds of millions a
real threat, the need to innovate was perhaps more urgent than
any time in history.

Combining his academic training, boyhood farmstead experience, and midwestern work ethic, Borlaug and his team invented a process called "shuttle breeding" that accelerated the
hybridization process dramatically. Shuttle breeding might
sound fancy, but it wasn't; it basically means the scientists carried the plants by hand from field to field, across regions,
mountain ranges, and climates and crossbred the plants by
hand. Turns out, there's no replacement for a hard day's work.

By leveraging Mexico's multiple growing seasons, the
Borlaug–Rockefeller Foundation teams were able to develop
strains of robust, disease-resistant wheat in a fraction of the
time anyone could have predicted. And proving that bigger
isn't always better, one of the main innovations was the

development of "dwarf wheat." When plants grow shorter they are less likely to fall over and die. It turns out, living plants grow more food than dead ones.

These simple ideas allowed Dr. Borlaug and the Rockefeller Foundation to coax changes out of plants in a few years that would have taken decades through the previously existing breeding processes. In about half a decade—which, as science goes, is the blink of an eye—yields of staple crops increased 500 percent.

The evidence shows that Borlaug's work and the work of colleagues who followed in his footsteps saved more than a billion people from starvation in the middle of the twentieth century. Serious scholars have determined that this Iowa native who you've likely never heard of is "the man who saved more lives than any other person who has ever lived."

I was impressed, to say the least. But walking around the Hall of Laureates, I also learned about the state of Iowa's truly remarkable past as a leader in agricultural innovation and humanitarian outreach. There are more recent stories, such as that of Governor Bob Ray, who I mentioned earlier as a governor-cum-mayor in Des Moines, and who ignited his own state's and then the country's work to welcome hundreds of thousands of refugees from Southeast Asia in the turmoil of the late 1970s and early 1980s. I also learned about the work of George Washington Carver, who began his education and research as Iowa State University's first African American student.

But I also learned that if there was one person in history competing for the title of the world's greatest humanitarian, he was from Iowa, too. This guy, you've heard of. You just probably don't know the whole story.

In the depths of the Great Depression, our president Herbert Hoover took the brunt of the blame for a massive national and global economic disaster. Just as Oklahoma City had become synonymous with the bombing or the Dust Bowl, Hoover's identity has become associated with the Great Depression. But before that, in the aftermath of World War I, he created a massive relief effort that brought food to the starving masses in Northern and Western Europe. Serious scholars have said that Herbert Hoover, like Borlaug, is the man who saved more lives than anyone else in human history.

This was a lot for me to take in before a speech I was about to give on the social and health impacts of bicycle lanes in a modest-density city. But I'm glad that I took the tour, because it taught me something really important about how cities need to tell their stories; they must learn how to embrace the past to better understand their futures.

In the days when almost every city was out there trying to unlock the riddle and become the next Silicon Valley, it seemed like more than a few leaders in Iowa and its capital city understood that, in the future, food would still be important to our lives and happiness. Agriculture is Iowa's strength, and trying to run away from it really wouldn't do anyone any good.

One leader who I think understands this well is the president of the foundation that gives the annual World Food Prize. He is the inspiration behind the effort to save the library building and create a really spectacular destination for leaders from around the globe to visit.

His name is Kenneth M. Quinn, and though he wasn't born in Iowa (he was born in New York and is a lifelong Yankees fan), his history as an Iowan dates back to his family's move from the Bronx to Dubuque when he was a young boy.

Ken Quinn is as impressive a person as he is charismatic. His twin talents of critical intellectual insight and creating powerful personal connections took him far in the world. After college and a master's degree, Quinn entered the U.S. Foreign Service, expecting to find his way into the finer life of diplomatic negotiations in the chandeliered salons of Paris, Geneva, and Brussels.

Instead, the State Department sent Quinn to Vietnam, where he found himself frequently in the line of fire and was the only civilian to receive the U.S. Army Air Medal—for commanding active helicopter combat missions in the fighting.

This was not exactly what he had signed up for, but as he tells it, he learned some deeply challenging lessons about how conflicts arise, what it takes to sustain peace, and what it means to be an American and a humanitarian in a complex and conflict-prone world.

One of the key lessons I recall him imparting had to do with the importance of roads: Access to agricultural markets has the power to change places and people's lives almost instantly.

Quinn's diplomatic career and public service is the stuff of legend—the kind that makes you wish there was a hall of fame for public servants. He served on Henry Kissinger's National Security Council staff and also as chief Vietnamese translator to President Gerald Ford in the final work to wind down combat and operations in Vietnam. And under President Bill Clinton as U.S. ambassador to Cambodia, he led our nation's response to ending the terror of the deadly forces of the Khmer Rouge. He is one of the most highly decorated foreign service officers of his generation.

After over thirty years of service, we would all understand if the guy had retired to a golf course or a beach somewhere. Or if he'd wanted to keep busy, he might have taken a job running a think tank or perhaps become the chairman of a major company and earn a couple million bucks a year for making phone calls and giving speeches.

Instead, he returned to his adoptive home state—where he started his second career building the World Food Prize from what was in its early days a nice annual program that Dr. Borlaug ran to shed some light on the accomplishments of a number of scientists who were doubtless doing God's work, but otherwise rarely entered the public eye.

Today the World Food Prize is by any real measure the world's premier conference and global gathering of leaders at the nexus of research, policy, and leadership in the fight against hunger and malnutrition. Every October more than a thousand leaders convene in Des Moines from dozens of countries and nearly every state in the United States.

And the building that calls this institution its home is the World Food Prize Hall of Laureates. The hall heralds the achievements of Iowa's "green" agricultural leaders that have led the way in feeding the world. Looking to a greener future, the building has become one of only a handful of century-old buildings to achieve LEED Platinum certification for its innovative sustainability and energy conservation. With this, the story of Iowa's hunger-fighting, humanitarian legacy can reach the people of Iowa a hundred years into the future.

Like the transformation of our riverfront in Oklahoma City that was for decades an eyesore into an amazing global asset, leaders like Ken Quinn and others around him turned the downtown library building—and the city's and the state's humanitarian legacy—from a liability into one of Des Moines's great treasures.

Maybe you've never heard of Norman Borlaug, or never knew that before Herbert Hoover was president, he organized the biggest food relief program in human history. Well, that's too bad and probably something that should change. But the main point is that your city's history is full of heroes and has a story that the people who live there need to know. It takes work and a unique ability to understand how retelling the past contributes to our future.

This may seem like a chapter about rivers. But the heart is a story about the ways that old buildings, eyesores, and old-fashioned industries can be refreshed to make your city great again. Sometimes traditions are the best foundation to build on. Your city has its untold stories that need to be told. And assets like our river and Des Moines's century-old library that need to be saved. And believe it or not, the world is listening.

CHAPTER 5

Making the Big Leagues

At the height of the August heat in 2005, New Orleans lay in a shambles. The massive storm had come and gone, but Katrina's waters had breached the levee and poured down into the city. Days after landfall, there was no sign of retreat.

Across the South, city halls far from the storm were pelted with frantic phone calls from desperate decision makers. Businesspeople who had planned conventions in New Orleans were scrambling to find alternatives. Businesses in the Big Easy were hoping to find office space and were willing to relocate, at least temporarily. Meanwhile the state of Louisiana and the federal government were preparing to put thousands of evacuees on buses and planes to destinations unknown.

As our staff worked on helping those in need, I remember thinking about the huge array of unpredictable repercussions that hit a city when natural disasters strike.

I looked at my watch. It was just after nine o'clock on a Wednesday morning—ten o'clock in New York. In between calls from FEMA and the breaking stories on the news, I asked my executive assistant to place a call to David Stern, then the NBA commissioner. Instinctively I knew that among the businesses that would be affected was the town's professional basketball team, the New Orleans Hornets. Maybe this was a place where Oklahoma City could offer something uniquely valuable.

I had been mayor for just a year and a half. And while my interest in pursuing a professional sports team for Oklahoma City was widely known, the fact that I had already made three trips to New York seeking a team was not. Making cold calls to league commissioners would have been deemed a laughable waste of time to 99 percent of the citizens of Oklahoma City. We were a minor-league city. That's just the way it was. Inside the city limits, we didn't even have a Division I basketball team. Geez, every city had Division I basketball. But not us.

We were capable of more and I knew it.

I probably love sports more than the average guy, but the reason I thought we needed a professional sports team went far deeper than that. I believed it would be the quickest and most effective way to improve our image. Our image needed help, both internally and externally. We were known mostly for tragedies, and it was holding us back. If only we could attach our city's name to a major-league sports team—something positive and exciting and fun. I really believed it would change everything.

Our Brand Is Disaster

In the years leading up to becoming mayor, I had spent countless hours studying the brands of different cities. What images came to mind when I said "New York" or "Seattle" or "Miami"? Maybe you have traveled to these places and have your own experiences to rely upon. Maybe not. Perhaps as I mention these cities, an image came to your mind anyway. A news story. A movie scene. Perhaps a television show—*Seinfeld* or *Frasier* or *Miami Vice*. More than anything else, television news and pop culture affect how we view other places.

And of course I thought about our brand, too. Inside the state of Oklahoma, people sensed the MAPS improvements would lead to good things. There were actually people living in our cross-state rival, Tulsa, that were impressed by what we had done. And in the multi-state region, word was beginning to spread that Oklahoma City was an improved place. But to most of the world outside of Texas, Kansas, and perhaps Missouri and Arkansas, Oklahoma City was still a forgotten dot on a map. The last time most Americans had thought about us was the day of the bombing—and those horrific images were deeply embedded.

And then another direct hit. Just four years later, in 1999, the skies opened up and a big, wide twister touched down along the southern edge of our city limits. The media predictably called it the "Oklahoma City tornado"—and our confidence, which we had pieced back together after the bombing, shattered one more time. Thirty-six people died. The national media returned with their satellite trucks. The dented brand of Oklahoma City took another hit. And again, people felt sorry for us.

By 2001, I was on the city council and trying to communicate to others inside of city hall how our brand had been destroyed and that we had to change it. We needed to build a stronger economy. We needed people from outside of Oklahoma City to invest in Oklahoma City. We needed people to want to bring jobs to our city. And most of all, we needed our existing companies to be able to entice talented people from all over the country to move to our city.

If someone in Boston or San Francisco got a job offer in Oklahoma City, were they going to think, "If I take this job I *have* to live in Oklahoma City"? Or were they going to think, "If I take this job, I *get* to live in Oklahoma City"?

We all knew the answer.

I was also amazed at how little we did in the city to improve our brand. Or, for that matter, *acknowledge we had one.* If you drove around the city in those days, the words "Oklahoma City" were almost impossible to find. It wasn't on buildings. It wasn't on signs. If we had passed a law that made it illegal to display the words "Oklahoma City," we could not have done a better job. If we had visitors—and we did have decent automobile tourism because of our three interstate highways—they had better know what town they were visiting, because we were not going to tell them! We weren't communicating with our audience about what we were or who we were.

In 2000, we got a top-level Arena Football League team. It certainly wasn't the big time, but with other franchises in New York, Los Angeles, and Chicago, it was a step forward. Sure enough, though, when the front office chose a team name, they wanted no part of attaching themselves to the fortunes of Oklahoma City. They became the Oklahoma Wranglers. A subtlety that most couldn't see.

There was much more evidence to consider. I soon learned that a lot of the opportunities to display the brand of our city fell upon our state's department of transportation, our airport, and our own public works department. These are organizations filled with engineers. Engineers are wonderful at building roads and runways, but they generally don't think much about communicating with the people driving on those roads and landing on those runways.

What's in a Name? Everything

In 2002, it was time to name our new sports arena. Even though it had been built with the capability of hosting an NHL or NBA franchise, our only tenant was a low-level minor-league hockey team. Therefore, the naming rights were not all that valuable.

When I learned late in the process that we had agreed to terms with the local Ford auto dealers to name it the Ford Center, I tried to get the city to reconsider. Nothing against Ford, but here was a chance to put *our* name on something. And after all, our citizens had paid for the thing outright.

Here was a chance to improve our brand by displaying our city's name on something positive. Why not call it the "Oklahoma City Sports Arena"? I was actually open to anything as long as the words "Oklahoma City" were in the name. Could I convince my colleagues that this was important?

I made a short speech in the council meeting explaining my thought process for turning down the money and keeping the name of the arena for ourselves. Then, our mayor asked for a motion to move ahead on the deal with the Ford dealers. We voted. I lost 8–1. My colleagues glared at me for wasting their time.

A year later, it was the second verse of the same song. This time we had made some significant improvements to our performing arts center. I suggested that when we reopened the building we should also rename it.

When the building had originally debuted in the 1930s, it was christened "Municipal Auditorium." When it was improved in the 1960s, it had been renamed the "Civic Center." Surely we could do better.

I suggested that if you made a list of the most bland and forgettable names possible, "Municipal Auditorium and Civic Center" would be near the top.

I further suggested we rename the building the "Oklahoma City Performing Arts Center."

This time I started earlier on gathering support. After losing the argument about naming the sports arena, I really wanted to make a point here: We have to look after our brand. No one is going to protect it if we don't. The media had picked up on my effort and it got some decent coverage. I met with the leaders in the arts community. I visited with the mayor and several members of the city council. My elected colleagues were receptive. The arts community had no reason to know who I was. I suppose I hadn't earned their respect. After all, in their minds I was probably just a sportscaster playing politician! What the heck did I know about art? They seemed offended that I had the audacity to weigh in at all.

By the time the issue came to a vote, the arts community had rallied its supporters to contact the city council representatives in an effort to stop me. It was a fairly heated debate. The council was torn. They could see my passion and, by now, wanted to support me. But the arts community was important to them as well. And these people donated to their campaigns. To most of the council, this seemed like a lot of controversy for nothing.

At the council meeting that would determine the outcome, the arts community stood its ground and spoke out against my resolution for the better part of an hour. Finally, I spent a few minutes making my pitch. Let's connect the city's name with something positive. The mayor was out of town so there were eight of us that would decide the outcome. I needed only four other members of the council to back me.

Rather than vote, the council first wanted to defer the item. This was an attempt to make the idea go away. But I was not interested in putting this off any longer. I had spent months pleading my case. Of course my pride was involved. I am human. But the point was more about our brand than the name of a building. And I was ready to move on.

We needed a vote, one way or the other. And how could the city's council vote against putting the city's name on a city building? Well, they did. The resolution failed in a tie vote 4–4. I was disappointed. I was a little bitter. But even in losing I had drawn attention to the issue. People in Oklahoma City were at least thinking about the city's brand for what seemed like the very first time.

Big-League City. At Least for a Year

Three years later, there I was in my office watching Katrina attack New Orleans. By then, a lot had changed. As mayor, I was often speaking passionately about Oklahoma City's emerging status. I talked about our assets and our strengths. Our civic leaders had accepted my stance on our underwhelming brand. They agreed it was an issue, though we still didn't seem to have a committed plan for how to address it.

Downtown had changed rapidly, and with cranes in the sky and steel on the ground, it was clear more change was on the way. We were moving an interstate highway, which would allow for a new park and a new boulevard. I secretly hoped we could rename the street "Oklahoma City Boulevard," but that opportunity was still a few years away.

NBA commissioner David Stern called me back around noon. He said he didn't call me right back—he knew what I wanted anyway, and he needed to do a little more due diligence on his end. But my suspicion was correct. Stern was already trying to determine if the New Orleans Hornets were going to be able to play in New Orleans for the upcoming season.

When I told him we had looked at the Hornets' home schedule and it appeared that thirty-five of the forty-one dates were available in our Ford Center arena, his positive feedback was telling.

"Really?"

It was obvious that, although my previous conversations with him about Oklahoma City getting an NBA team had not progressed, things had suddenly changed.

The commissioner and I were both concerned about the optics. We clearly weren't just looking to poach a team from a wounded city, and I was very concerned about the sensitivity of it all. Ten years earlier, it had been our city that was facing tragedy. I didn't want to look like we were taking advantage of New Orleans. The city of San Antonio was already being criticized for talking about relocating the NFL's Saints from New Orleans to Texas. And I didn't want to do that to my city or theirs.

But the chance to host real live NBA games in Oklahoma City was the opportunity I had been waiting for. An opportunity to brand Oklahoma City beyond its image as a place most people associated with terrorism or tornadoes. However, if it leaked to the media that I was in conversations with the NBA just days after Katrina, I could have rebranded Oklahoma City, all right—as a heartless community looking to take advantage of a city in peril.

Just six months prior, Stern had politely listened to my pitch and offered to help me attract major events or even an NHL team instead. My persistence earned me a nickname: "The

Mayor Who Wouldn't Go Away." But no matter how much he appreciated my passion on rebranding the city, he was always clear we weren't on the NBA's radar.

In fact, he couldn't have made it clearer. On my visit to New York in April 2005, he looked me in the eyes and emphatically said, "I don't have a team for you."

Just a handful of people within city hall had known about my conversations with the NBA over the previous year, and when we started talking about possibly bringing the Hornets to town, Stern and I insisted it remain a secret. But that Thursday night, the media caught wind of the story through a leak in the NBA's office.

Back in Oklahoma City, I spent the weekend convincing the governor and state leaders that we needed some help with incentives. They knew an NBA team would be an economic boon to the city. They also knew there'd be significant expenses for the team to relocate. I pushed state leaders to offer the same incentive we had used in our attempt to win the Big 12 basketball tournament. If the state didn't charge sales tax on tickets sold to the games, it would give the operator 8 percent off the top, which we estimated to be several million dollars.

State leaders agreed, and when I spoke to Stern again and mentioned the proposal, it showed how serious we were. He was talking to other cities and this set us apart.

By now, the story was growing. Opinions were mixed but there was a clear sentiment in the media and general public that this incredible, farfetched idea—that an NBA team could play almost all of its scheduled home games in Oklahoma City— might actually happen.

We were just six weeks from the beginning of the season. Usually, agreements between cities and leagues take months or years. Stern, the league, and the owners needed assurance that there wouldn't be any unnecessary political red tape or an arena full of empty seats on TV.

As is common now in post-MAPS OKC, business leaders stepped forward to help seal the deal. For the Hornets to agree to the move, the city, the state, and key investors like Aubrey McClendon and Clay Bennett had to take on the season's financial risk before tickets could even go on sale.

Clay Bennett was a natural salesman who had invested millions in Oklahoma City office buildings, so he knew almost everyone in the business community. He'd been instrumental in bringing an Olympic Festival to Oklahoma City in 1989, so his history of advocacy for sports in OKC was well established, too. When he went to business leaders ask their support for the Hornets, those leaders answered the call.

The league was stunned at the level of support that Bennett had put together in just a few days. The tickets he had sold and sponsorships he'd secured quieted any worries the NBA or the Hornets' organization might have had about a successful season in OKC. I was elated. And I knew there was a lot of work to do. We were in uncharted territory. In the history of American sports, no major-league franchise had ever relocated for a single season. No franchise has ever had only six weeks to gather corporate and fan support.

Stern assigned one of his top lawyers, Joel Litvin, to work with me on how our city would be branded in this unprecedented one-year experiment. The league initially didn't want to change the name of the team for just one season. I explained that if we really expected Oklahoma City to adopt this team as our own, we needed to put Oklahoma City into the team name.

The result was that the team would be called the New Orleans/Oklahoma City Hornets. Players would wear New Orleans jerseys on the road and Oklahoma City jerseys at home.

And the NBA's website, which used a three-letter abbreviation for all teams, would write NOK for the Hornets.

At this point, I was doing media interviews, explaining our city's concern over borrowing a team from another community—especially a community facing an enormous rebuilding process. To the extent that any city could possibly know what New Orleans was going through, we felt like we did.

"We are all a little uncomfortable with the way these events have transpired," I would begin in my talking points to our own citizens, who were trying to make sense of it all. "But I believe we need to support this team with everything we've got. Because at the end of this season, the world of sports is going to have reached a conclusion as to whether or not Oklahoma City can support a major-league sports team. And whatever that conclusion is, we will never be able to change it. This is our one and only chance."

Opening night seemed like the biggest night in our city's history. In the blink of an eye, a city that most Americans probably couldn't find on a map was the star of the show on ESPN. We had worked hard for this moment, and for the first time it felt like we deserved the attention.

At the first game, I looked around and sensed the energy in the crowd. It was surreal. It felt like the start of a four-month sports festival the whole city would attend. And at once, I knew it. We were going to make the most of our chance.

It was also the first time all of us OKC citizens stood united behind a single team. We had always embraced college football, but our loyalties were deeply divided between two teams. In our state, you were defined by whether you wore OU red or OSU orange on Saturday afternoon. Now, when the NBA came to town, everyone wore Hornets' purple and teal. Sports united us, rather than divided us. It was a powerful feeling that was just one of the unpredictable benefits of becoming a big-league city.

In New Orleans the year before, the Hornets hadn't won much. They finished the 2004–5 season a lopsided 18–64. In the off-season, the team drafted Chris Paul, a point guard from Wake Forest who would go on to become the NBA Rookie of the Year. Watching him play his first game—the first ever NBA game in our arena—I knew this was going to be a fun season. The Hornets defeated the Sacramento Kings, 93–67, and the crowd was on its feet most of the game. People were hooked, and within a month we were designated the loudest arena in the league.

At that point, David Stern flew to Oklahoma City to attend a game. It was actually the first time the commissioner and I had seen each other in person since our last meeting in his office in April. We recounted the bizarre series of events that had led to Oklahoma City setting a league record for corporate sponsorships and almost immediately selling out the entire season's worth of tickets.

The previous spring, Stern's words, "I don't have a team for you," had stung because they seemed so final. But here we were, seven months later, watching what felt like *our* team. At the end of that game, Stern announced that we were at the top of the relocation list.

That sounded great but, at the same time, it felt like no other team but the Hornets would do. The team and its players had become a real part of Oklahoma City. They hadn't been a sell-out in New Orleans, but here the place was full to the rafters night after night. The players loved it. They'd left their hometown not knowing what would happen, and they were grateful that Oklahoma City adopted them. Players did all kinds of community events to say thanks to our fans. One day, a six-foot-eight forward named Brandon Bass, who was born in Baton Rouge and studied at Louisiana State, brought cookies to my office to say thanks.

The city loved the team and the team seemed to love us back. When you've been a minor-league city for 115 years and you become a major-league city overnight, it's a dramatic change for your citizens. Now we were playing Chicago, New York, and L.A. It may not be fair, but on a superficial level your city gets a part of its identity by who your teams play. On a not-so-superficial level, people from other cities size you up differently when they see your name next to theirs on the score crawl across the bottom of the ESPN broadcast every night.

During that first year, the league realized the team couldn't go back to New Orleans right away. The city was still repairing its infrastructure and there was a concern that a damaged New Orleans could no longer support both an NFL and an NBA franchise. While the league and the Hornets ownership tried to figure it out, the one-year experiment was extended into a second season in Oklahoma City.

That second season would be the last. With New Orleans returning to normalcy, and the NBA lease still intact, the team needed to return. But by now, our citizens knew all the players and we were emotionally attached to them. To show how new we were to professional sports, when someone was traded we nearly came to tears.

And indeed, at the last game in Oklahoma City, I was choked up and so was most of the crowd. Our fans wept, knowing the team they had cheered for two seasons was leaving for good. The players, many of whom were only a year or two into their careers and had never played in New Orleans, didn't want to leave. On the night of their last home game, the budding all-star Chris Paul said, "This is definitely a city that I will never forget." And even ten years later, he still makes good on his promise to stay connected to the first NBA city he ever knew.

But leave they did. Our city had been changed forever. The national media repeated the remarkable story line over and over. Oklahoma City had proved it could support a major-league franchise and certainly another NBA team would be on its way soon.

The rest of that story was no easy task. From two time zones and two thousand miles away, Clay Bennett had created an ownership group that bought the Seattle Sonics. After a year of trying—and failing—to get a new arena built in Seattle, the league gave him permission to move the team to a proven market. Oklahoma City was at the front of the line.

After a season without basketball, we had just one final hurdle to clear, an initiative to improve the arena. So we passed a fifteen-month sales tax extension to fund improvements to our MAPS arena. And with that, OKC secured a long-term lease with the NBA.

There were more fights for our brand on the horizon. Once again, the league had a strong preference for naming the new team after the state instead of the city. I agreed we were a small market and it would be important to have a statewide identity. But as much as I appreciated their concern, by name this had to be Oklahoma City's team. The branding process had to complete its course.

It did. Though there were thousands more decisions and wrinkles to iron out, we could see the end of a long journey in sight. And the Oklahoma City Thunder took the floor in the fall of 2008.

Oklahoma City: World-Renowned and Proud of It

Every city and town across the United States has an image. What do people who live inside the city think of themselves? What visuals come to mind when people across your state think of your city? Do people across the nation even know your city exists? Is it in the news? Have events or pop culture created an image of your city that is flattering or unflattering?

Oklahoma City's former mayor Ron Norick tells a story of getting on an airplane in 1990 and having someone sit next to him and ask where he was from. "I'm from Oklahoma City," Ron said matter-of-factly. The reaction was just a blank stare. "It was like they didn't know what to say next," he said later. "They just had no perception of Oklahoma City."

And that story was not unique. No wonder we had trouble getting corporate America and fast-growing companies interested in creating jobs.

Things are different now. A woman came up to me recently to tell me that initially she hadn't understood why I'd worked so hard to get an NBA team. "Mayor, I want you to know that I get it now," she said. "When you were telling us to pass the sales tax, I supported you but I didn't think it was a big deal. But I was just in Turkey on a trip and the person picking up my bags at the hotel asked where I was from. When I said Oklahoma City, he said, 'Thunder!' " When a stranger in Turkey knew this woman's city, she knew what I had said was true. Her city was culturally relevant.

Perception matters. If you want capitalists from outside your city to invest in your future, it helps immensely if they enter the conversation with a positive impression. From the inside, if you want entrepreneurs and talented young people to remain in your city and help build that future, they need to feel good about your image and future, too.

The millennial generation is full of young people who want to live in a city that is culturally relevant. If that draws up an image of a nice art museum, fine. That's important. But keep in mind that what may be more important is having a connection to the outside world through MTV or ESPN.

How often is your city mentioned on national television shows? What cultural, political, or sporting events draw statewide or national attention?

Your city's current leadership is probably not responsible for how your city got its current image, but they must take ownership and recognize how important it is to attract the talent necessary to compete in the twenty-first century.

SACRAMENTO: CAN KEVIN SAVE THE KINGS?

A lot of the country's biggest metros have multiple sports teams to call their own. New York has so many they can make sure the names of most of their teams rhyme. They even occasionally export their teams to neighboring states when there's just too much to do in the Big Apple. This is not a problem that most midsize and smaller cities in America have.

There does seem to be a close relationship between how few teams a place has and the intensity of their fan base, too. And when a city is about to get their first or only pro team—or is on the verge of losing their big-league status—the ferocity of the fan comes out in full force. In no city or sports story is this principle clearer than the recent history of the Sacramento Kings. In particular the steps that NBA All-Star mayor Kevin Johnson, and I believe only Kevin Johnson, could take to keep the Kings in his hometown.

People love sports. Cities love their teams. And mayors are absolutely no different. Kunal Merchant, who served as Mayor Johnson's chief of staff during his first term in office, put it this way: "If you don't understand how important sports are in cities, just ask yourself if any other industry has a three-to-four-minute segment devoted to it in every local newscast."

A lot of tenured university professors of economics with a lot of letters after their names study the impact of sports on urban economies. Most have little positive to say—and they are especially skeptical when it comes to the question of whether stadiums are good projects for mayors to spend their time on. I've looked at the numbers, too, and it's not always clear cut. But the skepticism I see in the studies really seems out of step with what people are clearly perfectly willing to vote for and pay for.

We in Oklahoma City pretty obviously disagree with that line of thinking. We built what is now known as Chesapeake Arena without any big-name sponsorships lined up, and therefore without a name, and without even having a team to play in it yet. Showing just how important sports can be to a city and its voters, we built it all with taxpayer dollars and without a dime of debt.

Oklahoma City believes in sports. Economics aside, sports teams play a huge role in determining which caste your city belongs in. For OKC, getting the professional sports team was a city-defining moment. For Seattle, who we attracted the franchise away from, it meant a lot, but less in a city with two other professional teams and such a distinct global brand. Even so, I won't pretend that any time I talk to a Seattleite, I get at least a good ribbing about it.

A Mayor Whose Time Had Come

Kevin Johnson was born in Sacramento, attended and played ball at Cal Berkeley, and played out an all-star career in Cleveland and Phoenix. Johnson's time as a charter school star back in Sacramento always stuck in his mind, so after his career as an athlete, he decided to turn his attention to public service in his hometown.

When he was elected mayor in 2008, his city was reeling from the effects of the Great Recession: The foreclosure crisis was still in full swing and unemployment was high. The schools and infrastructure needed a lot of attention. And the state government's constant turmoil over taxes and regulation seemed to always hit a little closer to home in the seat of state government.

One glaring problem for the city's aim to stay a big-league city was the imbalance between the Kings' incredible fans and their arena's inability to do the kinds of business that newer arenas in other cities were now accustomed to.

In the background, everyone knew this imbalance would come up sooner or later, but the city loved its team so much that it didn't even come up much in the campaign. His predecessor had stayed neutral the last time the issue came up—and the measure had predictably failed. In fact, Kevin Johnson positioned himself in the campaign as more of a non-establishment leader with fresh ideas rather than an NBA star making a homecoming. The issue of the team never really came up.

Until it did.

At the NBA All-Star Game in 2011 in Los Angeles, NBA commissioner David Stern took a few minutes for a press conference and took a question from a reporter on the future of the Sacramento Kings. Under pressure, and without much warning or any fanfare, Stern let it be known that the Maloof family, who owned the Kings, were looking seriously at moving the team. Perhaps a little ironically, the likelihood was that the team would relocate to Anaheim, just a few miles away from the Staples Center, where the All-Star Game was being played.

Losing your standing as a major-league city is a big-league blow to any city. But in Sacramento, the bite would be particularly hard. For any mayor, right behind poor management of a major snowstorm, losing a professional sports team is a black mark on your résumé that it is very, very hard for locals to forget.

The NBA All-Star mayor was going to end up losing the city's NBA team? That couldn't be right. Mayor Johnson understood better than any other mayor probably could the importance of sports and the city. He knew he had to find a way to win.

The other major reason this just couldn't be true was how popular the team is in Sacramento. Maybe it's the name they picked but somehow that team and its players are Sacramento royalty.

For those of us out in the Midwest, the Kings are to Sacramento what the Packers are to Green Bay. In a way, maybe even more. The Kings had sold out almost every game in almost every season in their history—even across long stretches without a winning record. In fact, the Kings had sold out every game across nineteen of twenty-six seasons. And only seven of those seasons ended with winning records.

These are not your normal NBA fans. The team's presence and power in putting the city of Sacramento on the map was, and is, remarkable. So, right away, the mayor's team and city leadership sprung into action, engaging with the league and ownership to figure out what it would take to make this problem go away.

Now, the game of basketball has its own particular politics and priorities that are important to understand here. The league has specific—and high—standards for its markets and owners. The league is not interested in ownership that extracts profits to cover their living expenses. Teams should be profitable, sure, but the importance of a franchise's ability to contribute to the community is at least as strong as the bottom line.

And the ownership and the league protect these values by voting together to accept or deny petitions to change locations or to sell or buy a franchise. All that said, there is a lot of deference paid to owners for how—and where—they choose to run their businesses.

Knowing all of this, Johnson and the city approached the league to see what they needed to do. They knew they could rise to any challenge set before them, and the league laid out three basic bars they needed to clear to keep the Kings.

First, the league was concerned about the quality and viability of team ownership. This box was checked. Even if the Maloofs decided to sell, the Sacramento community had several local and national investors ready to step into their place.

Second, the league cared about the strength of the market and the quality of the fan base. This box was checked twice. Kings fans are among the craziest and most loyal in the league. And while Sacramento isn't the biggest market in the country, Commissioner Stern always had a soft spot for Sacramento and the league's smaller markets in general.

Third, the NBA cared about great arenas. The teams need to offer a great in-person experience as sports increasingly compete with hundreds of new choices for entertainment. Here, Sacramento faced its biggest challenge in keeping the Kings around.

An Arena Worthy of Its Team

The Kings' arena, historically known as ARCO Arena, was a problem. And getting public money for an updated facility (something the guys in Anaheim and several other places without teams were more than ready to throw in) is hard anywhere. But this was especially difficult in Sacramento, the state's capital city.

In California, raising taxes requires a public referendum in the state per the rules of the infamous Proposition 13. Raising taxes to fund a particular project? For that, you've got to go to the polls and win supermajority support. That had been tried in 2008 and was delivered an astounding 60 percent defeat at the polls.

To invest in their arena, and win the NBA's support to keep the team, they would have to find a way to finance the project without using tax dollars. Mayor Johnson would still need to secure council approval for the project, so they developed a plan that would fit the bill.

Mayor Johnson's team put together a really inventive package of ideas that dissolved the worry that residents who didn't love or care for the team would be effectively footing the bill for ballplayers' incredible salaries. In tight budget times, keeping a team in town shouldn't outweigh the delivery of core city services or push the cost onto the backs of hardworking families or people in need.

What they did have a lot of around the area downtown was another asset—one that doesn't sound exciting but in reality is a secret weapon for city innovation: municipally owned parking garages. Like sidewalks and schools and resurfaced streets, a lot of the magic of making a city great starts off in some pretty mundane places. In Sacramento, the key to saving the Kings and staying a big-league city was hiding in between stacks of concrete and a lot of parallel painted yellow lines.

Parking is a pretty reliable business, especially in the capital of the largest state government in the country. The city's garages had a good business already, but increasing their use at night with basketball games and concerts at the arena would make it even better. In California, passing a new tax to fund an arena would be a nightmare. But linking the funding directly to parking for the games? That might just work.

Of course, they needed the money that game parking would produce down the line to build the infrastructure now. So, they financed the project and sold those future revenues out to investors to back the plan. Game parking might be a little more expensive than usual because of this financing, but the city assumed that the locals would believe the deal was worth it. And they were right, because there's a pretty close correlation between the people who park for games and those who care about the team.

Now, you're probably wondering why on earth the city didn't just force the rich and fancy owners to reach into their pockets to build a new stadium for their Kings. Like we said before, the team had to be making money—and if these rich families have enough money lying around to pay their star players ten million a year, perhaps they should come up with some cash to improve the house their teams play in. Right?

Well, it turns out it's not that simple, and for a couple important reasons. First of all, there are a lot of cities out there that would bend over backward twice to get a good NBA team. Especially if you think about just how many large cities in the United States don't have professional sports franchises.

Second, we sometimes have to take into account the realities of the ownership families. In very few cases would it make sense for a person or family to own a pro sports team as their primary source of income. Even if the team does make money, it is part of a larger portfolio of projects in which the sports team is rarely the most profitable and is never able to solve problems in the owner's main lines of business like real estate, banking, and software.

It turns out that just that kind of situation was unfolding in Sacramento. The Kings ownership was a real estate family, and in the years following the recession and economic fallout of 2008 and 2009, their holdings took a major hit. For the ownership, saving the team might mean having to move it to a place where the stadium was brand-new and the business could more easily stand on its own two feet.

For Mayor Johnson and his colleagues, this project was about much more than pleasing sports fans. Keeping the Kings was the heart of a strategy to keep Sacramento's place as a big-league city, invigorate its downtown, create hundreds of jobs, and spark billions of dollars in economic activity. The value of sports teams goes way beyond the benefits to team owners and the leagues.

Readers in and around Sacramento might read this interpretation as being terribly favorable to the Kings' ownership. I am not taking sides, but the point I am trying to make is that even when there are the best intentions to remain loyal to a team's fans, reality can get in the way. And this is what happened in Sacramento.

Armed with these clever ideas, Mayor Johnson and the team put together an impressive package and garnered enough public support to put the idea into action. They again approached Commissioner Stern and the owners, and made clear what they were willing and able to do.

About eight months of waiting—an eternity in sports time—went by. But Kevin had learned, as I had over the years, that David Stern is a stand-up guy. If you are true to your word, he and the league will live up to their end of the bargain.

So the city—and, really, everyone—was pretty stunned when the Maloof family backed out of the deal and announced they were once again shopping for a new home. This time in Seattle, a city that had lost their team (to us) just a few years earlier.

Johnson knew he was in for a fight. To up the ante, they improved the stadium concepts—which were already inventive on the financial side—to serve as a major catalyst to reinvigorate a struggling part of the city and deepen the team's impact on the community as a whole. Just a few of the examples of their willingness to go above and beyond:

- The Golden 1 Center is entirely powered by solar energy and is the first arena to have earned a LEED Platinum rating for its environmental sustainability.
- More than 70 percent of the contracts for the work to be done were awarded to small and local businesses in the region.
- More than 90 percent of the food served in the arena is locally grown and sourced within one hundred miles of Sacramento.
- These jobs create immense opportunities for local residents, and the team works with local high schools and youth organizations to teach young people job and entrepreneurship skills through the snack sales during the games.
- The costs of any overruns or delays in construction would be borne not by the citizens of Sacramento but the team's ownership.
- They convinced the league and the ownership to sell the Kings to a group of more locally focused owners at a record valuation in NBA history.

Mayor Johnson's hard work paid off. And though the story was very different from ours in Oklahoma, I think about his effort almost every time I head to a Thunder game, just down the street from our city hall.

For other cities fighting to enter the big leagues, there are other opportunities—even outside sports—to enter the upper echelon of urban markets in the country. As Major League Soccer gains popularity and prepares a wave of expansions, a whole new set of cities will have to think hard about how to pay for a new arena for a team. When Oklahoma City plays your city on the basketball court or the baseball field, just know that while I might not be rooting for your team, I am certainly cheering for your city.

CHAPTER 6

Where Leaders Come From

I grew up in the rolling suburbs of Oklahoma City at the tail end of the baby boom. I was weaned on *Leave It to Beaver* and rarely missed *The Brady Bunch*. My life wasn't much different than those of the kids I was watching on television. By the mid-1960s, my parents, who had grown up during the Depression, had risen to the middle class. My dad delivered the mail. My mom taught first grade at a public school a couple of miles from home.

My grade school was around the corner from where we lived. I could walk or ride my bike about anywhere I wanted. It seemed like I was always going somewhere: the park, a friend's house, a nearby shopping center to buy baseball cards.

One thing that seems odd, though, as I look back, was that in the 1960s, dogs and cats roamed freely throughout the neighborhoods. Almost every house had a kid and almost every kid had a dog. The kids that didn't have a dog had a cat, maybe even several. I guess we were supposed to keep track of our animals, but with kids in charge, dogs got loose. A lot. And cats, well it is as difficult to keep cats in your yard as it is to teach them to fetch.

So, one summer day when I was probably seven, I picked up

a kitten that seemed to be wandering aimlessly up my street and, well, you know the rest of the story.

"Mom, can I keep it?"

We had "Dinky" (there was an unwritten rule that whoever found the stray cat got to name it) about ten years. Dinky was a friendly cat. Apparently, the other cats in the neighborhood thought so, too, because Dinky had kittens. How many times? I don't know that I remember. Twice? Three times? There were five to seven kittens in each litter. You get the picture.

Each time, the kittens would stay with us for a few weeks before we would try to find them a loving home. Cats had absolutely no value in our neighborhood, as they were seemingly everywhere. But my dad always insisted that I at least try to find someone who actually wanted a cat. So one time, when I took the litter to school for show-and-tell, a girl in my class surprised me and said her family was hoping to find a cat. That was a big deal. A successful adoption! That was the exception— the rule being that the kittens got a little bigger and about the time they gave up on nursing and wanted cat food, my dad announced that he was taking them to the animal shelter.

The first time this happened, I cried. I wanted to keep the kittens. But Dad explained the hard facts of kitten parenthood. Number one, we can't keep seven cats. Number two, the animal shelter will find people that want our cats. Now this wasn't exactly the same story that my friends were telling me about kittens going to the animal shelter but I knew my dad wouldn't lie, and it was the story I wanted to believe. After all, to me, these weren't just any kittens. These were really cute kittens that belonged to Dinky and me. They had names and personalities and I knew they were going to have long, great lives with some other families.

On departure day, my mom always insisted that Dinky was

watching as my dad loaded the kittens into a cardboard box and took them out to his car. Mom didn't want Dinky wondering what happened to her kittens and spending her days looking around the neighborhood for them. That made sense to me. Dinky was a good mother.

I remember Dad came home one day and recounted his trip to the shelter. He said that as he arrived, a little girl saw him walking in and proclaimed, "That's the kitten I want!"

It was a story I have told probably a hundred times. If Dad made up the story to make me feel better, good for him. Sadly, our family's story wasn't unique. Every year in the 1960s and 1970s, thousands of animals headed into the Oklahoma City animal shelter. And very few left alive.

Christy Counts: An Unlikely Hero

Christy Counts grew up in Oklahoma City a couple of decades after I did and a couple of neighborhoods away. Her childhood probably wasn't much different from mine, though. Her neighborhood was more affluent and her schools were private but as kids we probably had a lot in common. She, however, would grow up to help change everything about pet ownership in Oklahoma City.

As a kid, Christy was infatuated with dogs and cats and wanted to take care of every stray she encountered. At first her parents tried to accommodate her passion. They let her keep the first stray dog she found. And the second. And the third. But soon she was adopting an animal a month and her parents were overwhelmed. Some little girls wanted to dance. Some wanted to play with dolls. Christy was obsessed with saving stray dogs and cats.

One day her babysitter picked her up from school and offered to take her anywhere she wanted to go. That was a rare treat.

"You'll take me anywhere?"

No doubt the babysitter was thinking they would go get ice cream. Or maybe head to the shopping mall.

Christy could not have been more excited. "Let's go to the animal shelter!"

The animal shelter was her favorite place in the world. There, she got to visit and pet animals that had been pulled out of neighborhoods all across the city. She talked to them. If they were nervous and scared, she calmed them down. If they were mean, she provided kind words that seemed to improve their disposition. She was the Mother Teresa of the animal kingdom.

Christy went on to boarding school and eventually graduated from the University of Oklahoma. She traveled. Still in her twenties, as she pondered what to do next, she watched her classmates choose career paths they hoped would lead to fortune and fame. Christy was young, attractive, and educated. She had options.

So, she did what no clear-thinking, ambitious person would do. She applied for an entry-level job at the Oklahoma City animal shelter. Her stunned parents shook their heads in disbelief.

According to most normal measures, this was a really bad job. It basically paid minimum wage. And the shelter was definitely not a scene from *Leave It to Beaver*. It was overcrowded with multiple animals stuck inside each cage. Its concrete floors and cinder block walls smelled horrible. It was extremely noisy. And it was depressing.

It was mostly dogs and cats that entered the shelter. They would live uncomfortably for a few weeks, and then receive their death sentence. Their only crime was being born. Morale amongst the shelter's employees was understandably low. And the place was understaffed because every time there was a budget shortfall at city hall, the animal shelter was the first place the council felt safe making cuts. Most of the staff didn't like their jobs. They might have liked animals but that didn't mean they liked their jobs. And they didn't like Christy Counts.

She was different from the rest. It was clear that she came from a well-off family. And though the animal shelter was a pretty terrible place, she seemed happy to be there. So, in some subtle and not-so-subtle ways, they were mean to her. But still, every day, she came to work.

This was around the same time that I was elected mayor. One of the cold, hard facts I had to learn about city budgets is that there is no extra money to change the culture of the animal welfare department. City budgets—not just ours, but basically all of them—are built around the premise that the top priority is providing for public safety.

When budgets are lean, we as policymakers do whatever is necessary to protect the police and fire departments from budget cuts. And in the good times, when the tax base has relatively small, incremental increases, you give the men and women who put their lives on the line small raises. That's the priority. It's not that the people who fix the potholes and crawl around in the sewers aren't important, they simply don't get treated as well as those in the police and fire departments. That's just the way it is.

The result is that, through the years, other important services like street maintenance and park departments have to be more and more creative to maintain their service level. And lesser priorities, like animal welfare, never seem to get the attention they need. Unless a city has a really strong, growing economy, lower priorities like animal welfare are basically doomed. Oklahoma City was no different.

When I looked at the number of animals we were euthanizing at the animal welfare department, I was astonished. And sickened. I didn't see anyone working on it, and the numbers were getting worse and worse because the budget was getting smaller and smaller.

I was surprised that people weren't marching in the streets, because everyone who knew the extent of the problem felt the same way that I did. But there wasn't an easy solution—as any city could testify. We were probably one of the worst in the country, but it wasn't *much* better in most other places. How could a civilized society allow this to happen?

I learned that the cities who were having the most success were getting a lot of help from the private sector. We were getting a little help from donations but not enough to make a difference. When I talked to potential philanthropists—people who could make a real difference if they wanted—there was a recurring theme. They didn't have any confidence in our animal shelter. They didn't seem to think a little more money was going to change the culture. It was so underfunded, and so embarrassing, that it was hard to find people who wanted to be associated with it. Who could blame them?

Wealthy people are presented with endless opportunities to help society deal with its social concerns. Hunger. Homelessness. Poverty. Mental illness. The list of needs is long, and animal welfare is often easy to ignore.

I had a strong interest in helping to fix our problem but I really didn't have a plan. I had a lot of conversations about it, but they weren't leading anywhere. I was getting desperate. One day I asked the woman running our animal shelter if she knew anyone who might be able to rally the private sector to help us.

She said that if I was serious, there was someone she'd like me to meet. "There is a new person who works for us who might be able to help."

An Unusual Advocate for the Least Among Us

A week later, Christy Counts walked into my office. As we were talking, I was trying to figure it all out. She seemed too good to be true. More a rising star than entry-level employee, she knew how bad the problem was and still had confidence that she could make a difference. Obviously, she was committed to the cause and—just as important—she knew the philanthropists in town. She had grown up in that social network. But philanthropists and faith-based organizations usually spent money on life-and-death social issues like homelessness and hunger.

I explained the obvious to Christy: People of means surely wished the situation with the animal shelter was better and that fewer animals were killed. But they didn't want to throw money at problems when they didn't see a path to success. Just to be nice, I asked if she could rally their support. That was on a Friday.

By Monday morning, Christy was back in my office and she wasn't alone. She had spent the weekend making phone calls. The people in our community that had the ability to make a difference were ready to get involved. The cavalry had arrived. All I had to do—and this was very important to them—was pledge my support and promise not to use their success as an excuse to cut our existing animal welfare budget.

In other words, what they really needed was to be able to go to potential funders and say, "The mayor is supportive. And all of the dollars we raise will be additional dollars dedicated to saving the lives of dogs and cats in our community."

I gave my word, and Christy and her team went to work. They raised money and quickly allocated the funds to improve the lives of defenseless cats and dogs. The work they did on the private side relieved pressure from the city's Animal Control units, and they put themselves to work in some pretty creative ways.

Christy soon resigned her low-level position at our animal shelter and began work on what would become the Central Oklahoma Humane Society. With the added funds, the Humane Society was able to launch a marketing campaign to place pictures of sweet puppies and adorable kittens on television and in newspapers.

They started mobilizing spay/neutering plans, creating mobile clinics that went into struggling neighborhoods. Those efforts really helped reduce the number of animals that ended up in trouble in the first place. Both at the Humane Society and in the city's own facilities, the added capacity made it easier to keep the places clean and amenable to guests that might want to adopt.

You know what happened next. Little kids who loved animals like Christy and I had when we were kids said, "Mom, Dad, can we have one?" People started showing up and adopting animals.

Fairly quickly, the cages weren't so crowded and the animals were more comfortable, so even the anxious ones settled down and became less anxious and more adoptable.

In its very first year, the campaign was so successful that the city's animal shelter ran out of animals completely. Every single stray in the city had been adopted. And Christy and her team made sure everyone knew it.

The story ran on the evening news and in the newspaper, adding to the momentum. Of course, more cats and dogs arrived the next day but they no longer had to live in crowded cages. And being in the shelter was no longer a certain death sentence. When people came to the shelter, it was a more pleasant place and they were more likely to take an animal home.

Since the organization opened in 2007, they have found homes for over 25,000 cats and dogs and, perhaps more importantly, spayed and neutered over 115,000 animals. Stop for a moment and think of the magnitude of those numbers. Two thousand adoptions, and ten thousand surgeries happening every year on what is really a budget supported by the generosity of a few people following Christy Counts's lead.

Within a few years, the entire culture of animal welfare has changed in Oklahoma City. Christy and the people she recruited raised millions of local dollars and leveraged money from national grants that we would never have been able to access without their efforts.

Christy doesn't like to take the credit for our success, but the work she initiated has grown tremendously. An incredible number of people have volunteered and donated money. And every time I thank Christy, she points out, "We still have a long way to go."

But our improved animal welfare department and the coordinated effort with the Humane Society has made a world of difference. And it is still getting better. The entire culture of our community concerning animal welfare is much different. We raised the standards for how stray dogs and cats would be treated in Oklahoma City.

As mayor, I couldn't do it alone but I could support and empower Christy Counts. I could help by standing up and saying this is important.

Why was Christy Counts successful? There are a lot of factors, to be sure. But her passion and commitment to the cause were impossible to ignore. People could sense it, and they got on board.

There are people in every community with similar passion and commitment to an overwhelming social cause. Finding them, empowering them, and unleashing them to take on the big problems is a challenge for us all as we go forward.

BUFFALO: A PERFECT ADVOCATE
FOR AN IMPERFECT PLACE

Christy Counts is an interesting case in urban leadership that falls into an increasingly important zone between what we used to call the "public sector" and "charity." But as the line between public and private work has begun to blur, a number of outstanding leaders like Christy have found or created space for some pretty powerful ideas and their unique combinations of skills to take hold.

It seems there is an inverse relationship between the depth of the challenge and the height of creativity that leaders rise to in order to help, especially in cities that have reached points of economic or cultural desperation.

One city with such a story of leaders that seem genetically engineered to solve the challenges at hand is Buffalo, New York. The story centers on one of its "unofficial mayors," a gentleman named Pat Whalen.

Pat is a charismatic and interesting character—one of those people with a compelling presence who is focused on you and the issue that needs resolving but is equally willing to get out of the way when it is someone else's time to shine. In that Reagan-esque spirit of working hard whether or not he gets the credit, Whalen has worked on a variety of big projects over the years.

At this point in what probably is his third (but I seriously doubt his last) career, Whalen is working on a difficult and ambitious project to invite job creation and entrepreneurship in the hospitality and tourism industries in nearby Niagara Falls, New York.

I'm sure you've read about Niagara Falls, and I'm sure it

holds a fairly specific place in your mind. The falls are a powerful natural phenomenon located right on the border between
the United States and Canada. The place conjures up an image, at least for me, of a time in a younger America when being
the first man, or woman, or even little dog, to go over the falls
in a barrel and survive was national news. Later, before flights
to Europe, the Caribbean, and the South Pacific became easy
to arrange, Niagara Falls was the Honeymoon Capital of the
World. If you're old enough, or a fan of old movies, you might
even think of the falls in their heyday pictured in the Marilyn
Monroe thriller *Niagara* from 1953.

If you've actually been to Niagara Falls in the past couple of
decades, you probably have another image in your head that
conjures up a comparison to Dickens's classic *A Tale of Two
Cities*. Today, on one side of the falls, we see a vibrant, well-
appointed and well-traveled tourist destination with a variety
of activities for tourists of all ages. On the other side, we see a
city that is full of hotels and things to do but has definitely
seen better days. Unfortunately for us, and probably out of step
with our expectations, the sad part of the story is happening on
the United States' side of the falls.

Enter Pat Whalen. Pat is the kind of guy who sees potential
in everything—including himself, as you'll see—but the important thing for now is that Pat looked across Niagara Falls,
New York, and saw a city ripe for growth and innovation. "If
any place is hungry for change, it's Niagara Falls," said Whalen. "And I thought maybe I could do something about it."

Just a few years earlier, Pat had come out of an early and
well-deserved retirement to stoke the fires of innovation in a
struggling (and therefore high-potential!) city: his hometown
of Buffalo, New York.

For about ten years before turning to tourism in Niagara,

Whalen had been one of Buffalo's biggest advocates. The bulk of that time he'd spent as the COO for the Buffalo Niagara Medical Campus (BNMC), a project across government, healthcare, and business to build a "medical district" around several of the city's hospitals and universities. The medical campus was doing just fine moving existing jobs and doctors to a centralized location. But as Pat is still fond of saying, if all they did was relocate hospitals and jobs, they were just re-arranging the deck chairs on the *Titanic*. What was needed was *new jobs*. Jobs that could only come from an ambitious citywide effort to grow the potential companies and budding entrepreneurs in their midst.

You can probably imagine all the so-and-so's around Buffalo privately thought that this guy was crazy. *Buffalo, a startup and entrepreneurship hub? We can barely keep the lights on!* The city had been shrinking for years, and people were just going to have to get used to the fact that the population would continue to dwindle as families retreated to the suburbs, and college and high school grads zipped away to greener pastures as soon and as fast as they could.

But to other people, the challenge of sparking entrepreneur-ship in a shrinking city sounded like a great idea, and Pat and his colleagues decided to get to work. If you Google "Startups + Buffalo," you'll see what I mean.

Or, take a look at *Inc.* magazine's 2017 commentary on the city's strengths: It serves as a nicely located hub city, proximate to New York City, Toronto, and Chicago. The architecture is incredible—and, for serial entrepreneurs, the low-cost environ-ment and access to talent from SUNY Buffalo, the medical school, and several private colleges makes it a great place to grow your business.

The fact is that, by hook or crook, the city has started to

attract real numbers of millennial college grads looking for a city where they can get in on the ground floor of something big. Whatever the impact of all of this over the long run, the brain drain from Buffalo has slowed considerably. The town has a serious buzz about it, and on the biggest scale the central city's population decline—which had been under way for a couple decades—seems to have stopped, or perhaps even reversed.

This is important. For lots of cities, the goal need not be so far-reaching as managing million-person growth or figuring out how to bring in billions in investments. The tipping point that Buffalo has come close to reaching is re-establishing growth and trusting that their new residents will bring with them a vision for making their city an amazing place.

But even that isn't the most important point to make here. Really, the lesson to learn is the importance of finding and supporting the kinds of leadership that get these stories started, and then getting people working together to make them come true.

So, where do leaders like Pat Whalen and Christy Counts come from? It's complicated to describe, but I actually think it's very easy to find. Whalen and Counts come from very different places and walks of life. First, let's look at how they are different in order to see how much these two—and the people you should be hunting for—have in common.

Christy Counts was young and determined. She could have lived anywhere she wanted and perhaps gone to any school in the world. Pat Whalen could do whatever he wanted, too. But their backgrounds and the arcs of their lives and careers are quite different.

The first place I'll point you to is what Pat was up to before becoming the COO of the medical campus and its entrepreneurship programs. That was a big, important job that took some impressive interviews and professional accomplishments to land. If you peeked at Whalen's LinkedIn profile, you'd see that in the years before his university gig his title was "Ski Bum" and his employer "Any Ski Resort."

In his first career, Whalen spent about thirty years in the shipping and logistics business. He held senior management roles with the biggest name in the industry, UPS, and before that built his own companies to support the mega-firms, which he eventually sold to UPS for a pretty sound profit. Those kinds of accomplishments get you hired as a "Ski Bum" at the tail end of thirty years of work, I guess.

Whalen was a pretty accomplished guy before he started working to reinvent the tourism industry in Niagara Falls, and before he ran operations and led a turnaround for one of the biggest medical colleges in the country. Before he hit the slopes, he had built multiple businesses and executed an entire career in shipping and logistics. Any one of those three could be a legitimate life's work. So, where did this guy come from? What type of education and training did he receive to get his start in the world? What is the family legacy and connections he built upon?

Whalen never finished college. Not even close. He jokingly points out that he only ever passed one college class, Hockey 101. (Which is especially funny given he's teaching at Niagara University now.)

His family was a great support system, but hardly the kind that made all the high places low. Pat built things for himself and for his neighbors and friends. He worked for UPS as an early-morning truck loader to pay his tuition and figured out quickly that he made more money on that job than lots of people who had left school with a degree.

In a way, Pat Whalen and Christy Counts have almost nothing in common with each other except everything that matters.

To get started, they both had enough sense of what they love and care about, which included people and their cities and things like animals and startups that inspire them to work hard and dream big. They had confidence. They were driven.

It is people like these two who make our cities great. Many of them might have grown up or gone to college in your town and have relocated to other places to make money or work a job. For some of them, wherever they are, they are seeking an opportunity to go a step above and make a life—and that can be done in your cities, too. The key is creating a culture in which reasonable risks are rewarded and talent is applied where it can make the biggest difference. In changing places for the better, we can not only find, but can help create, the kinds of leaders our cities need to flourish. And great leaders can come from some pretty surprising places.

CHAPTER 7

Putting the City on a Diet

n what I like to call "a collective lapse in judgment," the voters of Oklahoma City elected me mayor in 2004. Perhaps I was a little naïve. And for an assignment at this level, I was certainly untested. But I was also energetic and optimistic. I sensed big things were ahead. It seemed to me the city was ready to tap into its hard-earned reservoir of strength and emerge as a new economic powerhouse. A lot of the MAPS projects had dramatically improved the quality of life and it showed equally in the headlines and on people's faces. We were a city on the verge of something great.

New people and great companies in dramatically different industries and walks of life wanted to visit—and make a home in—Oklahoma City for the first time in a long time. Oklahoma City was becoming a better place.

To validate all this as I started traveling across the country, I noticed that my city started showing up on those "lists" I talked about in the opening pages of the book. Magazine editors and webmasters love to promote and rank cities and, without really doing much about it, Oklahoma City was starting to show up on those lists. Now, at that time we weren't anywhere close to the top, but we'd been ranked fifteen or sixteen on Best Place to Get a Job or number twenty on *Forbes* Best Place to Start a Business. But hey, like Steve Martin in *The Jerk*, we were "somebody"!

This was all new to us. We were accustomed to being at best ignored or at worst maligned. But all of a sudden, there was a spark of energy in Oklahoma City. And to drive the point home, I used every list I could as often as possible when speaking locally to tap into and drive that emerging energy. We needed to believe in ourselves. We needed to believe that all the investments and hard work and compromises we had collectively made were about to take hold.

At the national level, I was starting to get some speaking engagements to talk about our schools' investments or our new arena. And again to drive the point home, I turned to "the lists" to make the case plain. Oklahoma City was no longer a second-tier place that people avoided and moved away from. We were a city to watch.

And then, thanks to *Men's Fitness*, came the list no mayor wants to be a part of: The Fattest Cities in America. And there we were.

Suddenly, the mayor who had been using these lists to validate the city's ascension was having to explain or defend why Oklahoma City had one of the worst obesity rates in the country.

Most cities, at this point, would go into a state of denial. Even the smartest, most reasonable people will twist themselves in knots to suggest that the data was collected unscientifically or that it's misleading or somehow, anyhow, disqualify and disregard the coverage.

Among citizens and leaders in Oklahoma City, though, the reaction was even more confounding. When we were placed on the list of the most obese cities in the country, it was hard to find anyone even trying to deny it. We just kind of looked at each other, nodded with crooked smiles, and said, "Well, I bet that's right."

The Elephant in the Room

It's not that we weren't aware of the problem. We could see it every day. We were bigger. We looked at our kids, and they seemed larger than the generation of kids who came before them.

One day at a pizza parlor, I noticed some kids dipping their pizza in ranch dressing. It was a visual that stayed with me. Our eating habits were becoming horrendous.

We all knew something was wrong. But apparently, we didn't have interest in doing a whole lot about it. We had some well-meaning anti-obesity efforts under way, but these programs seemed to have very little penetration among the rank and file.

Then I did something that really changed my mind and got me to work on this. I got on the scale.

I weighed 218 pounds. Seemed like a lot. Just to be sure, I went to a government website. I typed in my height, five feet ten. And I typed in my weight. And I hit enter. And when the results came up, my laptop screen said, "OBESE."

I thought, *What a stupid website! I'm not obese! I would know if I was obese!*

After the denial faded away, the meaning of that list hit home. After all, I now knew that I was part of the problem. Before the list came out, I suppose my approach had been, "Yeah we have a lot of overweight people in our community. Probably they should lose some weight." But I had never seen myself as part of the equation.

The good news is that if you're part of the problem, you can be part of the solution. I had lost weight several times in the past, and I knew I could do it.

As I started to examine my own history, I noticed that in my adult life I had developed a pattern. I would gain two or three pounds a year. And then about every ten or fifteen years I would get fed up and take twenty or so pounds off. Because of that, I had confidence that I could lose weight if I just devoted my attention to it, so that's what I decided to do. But this time it wasn't just about me. If I was working to change the city's image, I needed to be a better representative of the city and our state. Even if I couldn't change the city's health statistics, I could at least be a better role model.

The plan was pretty simple. I cut calories and started playing tennis again. But just because the plan was simple, that didn't mean it was easy. It seemed like everywhere I went, people were offering me food. Everyone wants to feed the mayor, and the mayor was eating!

I was eating about three thousand calories a day. I cut the calorie count down to about two thousand a day, and the pounds came off. In 2007, I lost about a pound a week for forty weeks.

During that process, the *Men's Fitness* list was never far from my mind. Why was it that Oklahoma City had perhaps the worst problem with obesity across the United States? What was it about our culture that made this an unhealthy place to live?

It seemed to me the first logical and necessary step was to just start talking about it. You see, Oklahoma City's weight problem had become one of those topics that polite people just didn't discuss.

Obesity affects the way people look, and it's just not considered polite to talk negatively about the way people look. So, our unannounced and unconsidered strategy for dealing with our obesity and all the health and social problems that came along with it was to just ignore it. Hey, maybe it would go away on its own!

Obviously that denial was getting us right where you'd expect it to get us. If we were going to change people's attitudes properly, I thought, "I've got to get a conversation going about this. How do I do that?"

The first issue was that in Oklahoma, city government covered a lot of bases but it didn't really get involved in health-related issues. That was for county government. So, whatever program I started wouldn't have a budget. That kinda limits your options.

If I had tried to get my colleagues involved, I'm sure I would have heard, "That's just not what city government is for!" or "City government is about potholes and police and fire, parks and court systems, and maybe animal welfare." "Health is not our mandate!" they might have said, or "The county has a board of health. They handle health. We handle other things."

And all of that was true.

I knew from the beginning that this project would be bigger on message and lower on budget. And luckily, one thing I knew how to do in the absence of money was to get the media talking. I knew I could come up with some way to make this into a story that reporters could write about and point a camera or two at. I just had to make it "interesting."

After thinking about it for a couple of months, I finally had an idea that I liked. I would announce that I was placing everyone in Oklahoma City on a diet. It was a little outrageous. But it was also a little whimsical. I wanted to make the program fun because losing weight is definitely not fun. And I felt like it would accomplish our goal: It would get people in Oklahoma City talking about obesity.

That's when I caught another break. I was having dinner with a friend of mine named Tom Michaud, the founder of Foundation HealthCare, an organization that owned and operated surgically focused hospitals. Out of the blue, he told me that he was ready to make some changes in his business and at that time in his career, wanted to give something back. Tom had been really successful and wanted to do something for the betterment of the community, but he didn't really know what to do.

The idea was right in front of me. I said, "Well, Tom, that's amazing. I have this idea to put the whole city on a diet, and I need some help pushing the idea out into the community."

In fifteen minutes, I told him about the plans that I was dreaming up for a website where people across Oklahoma City could sign up and log in once a week or so to keep track of the amount of weight they had lost. We would monitor the number of people who had signed up, and how many pounds they had shed.

Immediately Tom said, "Well, look, why don't I just help you do that?"

Rather than dream up his own project and start from scratch, he figured we could work together. So Tom gave some money and assigned one of his teams to build the technology. Tom had the website built extremely quickly and assigned one of his top IT people—a guy named Mike Panas—to work with me on the details.

We were getting closer and closer to launch, and I was starting to get concerned that virtually no one in our city's leadership had any idea what I was up to. Our health and weight statistics were truly just horrible. And here I was planning to draw attention to it.

This was no small issue for us, keep in mind. We had already lost United Airlines and God knows what other opportunities because of the quality of life in our city. What if shining light on a weakness like this drove even more potential future opportunity away?

I needed a gut check. I called Greater Oklahoma City Chamber president Roy Williams for advice. Like me, he was two or three years into his job, and he and I had worked together on a lot of the best things that had happened, including bringing a couple thousand Dell jobs and the Thunder to the city.

I wanted to give him a heads-up about what I was planning to do, without giving him all the details. I didn't necessarily need him to check with his board of directors or anything like that. I was trying to avoid promising too much while still taking the city's temperature from someone I trusted. I mentioned that I was working on an effort to get the city to lose weight—and I'm sure I undersold it. He said the business community would be all for it.

I told a few other people what I was working on and some of the feedback I was getting was that this was a really bad idea, at least politically. Risk-averse politicians are used to telling people what they want to hear. Here I was, planning on telling people the last thing they wanted to hear. I mean, who wants to find out they've been put on a diet? The only thing worse might be to announce to every voter that they would be getting a root canal.

I mentioned it to one of my closest political advisors and he said point-blank, "Don't do it."

It became very clear that this whole idea was running right across normal political instincts and rules of engagement. I don't recall any of my staff using the term "political suicide" but I'll bet it crossed a few people's minds—and potentially even their lips, behind my back.

It was definitely a departure for me. During my tenure on city council and in my first years as mayor, I can remember in neighborhood meetings and conversations that people would ask me about health. Every time, I took it as an opportunity to explain to them that city governments do *this*, state governments do *that*, and the federal government does something else. I used questions about health as an opportunity to give a speech on the responsibilities of different levels of government. That was a lot easier than actually answering their questions or addressing their deeper worries.

Then I started to change my perspective. Especially after I became mayor, I came to the conclusion that I was defining my job responsibilities according to the bureaucratic categories that had been explained to me by my colleagues. But in truth, my boss was really the voters that elected me.

The citizens of Oklahoma City thought that I should be working on health. The more feedback and questions I got on the issue, the more I realized that maybe I didn't get to prescribe, and maybe history doesn't define, what the mayor's role is in health.

I couldn't ignore my core responsibilities, of course, but if an issue comes up again and again, perhaps my job as mayor is to listen and assume the responsibility.

Enlisting the Elephants, and Ellen, and Everyone We Could

We called a press conference for December 31. Not exactly a day the press wants to be called out to work, but I knew the story would get a lot of play. It was the right thing to do.

We had the sense that this was really important to people, even if they wouldn't admit it publicly. We had a way for those people to participate and make the story last past the New Year's cycle. But it needed something else. We needed a visual. I decided to host the press conference at a place not many people visit over the holidays: the Oklahoma City Zoo.

I picked the zoo in part because I didn't want the "diet" to sound heavy-handed or negative. I could have stood in front of a cemetery and talked about all the people that had died because of poor health. I could have called the media to a city hospital, looking very official with doctors and nurses standing behind me, and talked about how many dollars obesity sucked out of our local economy every year. Both of those ideas seemed like downers to me.

I knew that this diet needed to be fun. And funny. And something we could rally around in a positive way. I wanted to take this negative health statistic, which was probably rightly something to be ashamed of, and turn it into a sort of rallying point for the city.

The team at the zoo was really excited about it, too, but all I had really shared with them was that I wanted to do a press conference in front of the elephants. Then, the day before the launch, the zoo team made a really important point to me: Elephants aren't fat. Or at least ours weren't.

They wanted to make sure I wasn't saying that our elephants

are unhealthy, fat, and overweight. Even though the elephants are *big*, they aren't necessarily *fat*. I have to admit that was the joke that I had in mind, but looking back it was a really important lesson.

We then altered course and said the elephants represent the size of the problem we're dealing with. Zoos have a lot of small animals, too, we thought, so I suggested we bring in some sort of small animal to which I could compare the elephant. The zoo brought along a ferret that I could hold in one hand.

I don't have to spell it out any more, do I? Currently our obesity issue is the size of these elephants and we are going to lose weight and be as slim as this small, sleek ferret. That's the goal.

I announced, "This city is going on a diet. And we're going to lose a million pounds."

The website had nutritional information and was designed to capture the email address of everyone that pledged to lose weight. And as they returned to log in their success, the website captured the number of pounds that had been lost.

Truth be told, Tom Michaud, the team, and I had agreed on a six-month effort on this campaign. If no one was signing up, or nobody was losing weight, we would give it six months, pat ourselves on the back, and move on to the next projects that came our way. Worst-case scenario, if all I had done was found a creative way to respond to the natural mandate I had gotten from my neighbors and voters, that would have been enough.

The press conference was on a Monday. Local television, radio, and newspapers did a number of stories that day and on Tuesday but by Wednesday, the immediate hit was dying off a little bit. Interest was waning. The website had some traffic but nothing astounding. But then there was Friday.

On that day, a local Associated Press writer named Jeff Latzke wrote a story about me putting the city on a diet. This wasn't an easy story to tell. But he captured everything about the issue really well, including the tone of the effort. And that's when the story took on a life of its own. The national media immediately began calling the Oklahoma City mayor's office.

This kind of attention is great but it can be as big of a shock as it is an opportunity. My executive assistant at the time, Gayleen Keeton, had spent several years at city hall, and before that she'd worked at the fire department and other city agencies. All of a sudden, Gayleen was fielding calls from television producers in New York and Los Angeles, who were inviting the very official-sounding "Mayor Cornett" to be on their shows.

The game had obviously changed.

In one meeting, Gayleen told the team, "Okay, we've got three national shows that want you to come on. But all of them are saying that they have to be the only one on which you appear. You definitely can't be on all three."

All three what?

I remember she said there was *The Martha Stewart Show, Rachael Ray,* and *The Ellen DeGeneres Show.* I didn't watch daytime TV and I remember thinking: "Oh, that's right. Martha Stewart is out of prison. She's back on the air?"

Next under consideration was Rachael Ray's show. I knew Rachael Ray was famous, but I didn't know why. I had seen her face on magazines at the newsstand, but that's about it.

Then Gayleen said that the next in line was *The Ellen DeGeneres Show.* "Ellen DeGeneres has a talk show?" I just thought she was a stand-up comic.

So there we were, me and Gayleen, trying to figure this out. Typically the issues we discussed were pretty ordinary, and suddenly Gayleen was my talent agent. Still, we had to make a decision. In the end, it came down to the basics: We did some research and *Ellen* had the biggest audience.

That is how I wound up on *The Ellen DeGeneres Show* with Taylor Swift. And that decision turned out to be beneficial in more ways than one.

After that taping, *The Oklahoman,* our city's major newspaper, ran a big front-page picture of me on the set with Ellen. The editorial team decided to carve out page-two space to start tracking the website totals on a daily basis. How many people had signed up? How many pounds had we lost?

The Oklahoman's commitment to document our success day after day was another breakthrough.

The story was picking up, one national report would lead to another, including *Time* magazine, which published a weekly quote from me on the campaign. What I didn't predict or expect was that this work would cross over into pop culture in some meaningful way. I thought it would be more of a serious news-and-health story, the kind of technical-sounding thing that the city blogs or Brookings Institution or the Pew Charitable Trusts might pick up on. But this mainstream attention was driving a ton of local traffic to the website.

Another upside of going on *Ellen* was that it set the tone: The city diet was covered as something fun, all about people in the community supporting each other. It was seen as *positive*. We'd taken this thing that we had been ashamed of and we were doing something about it.

That's how this negative story became a national narrative. Other cities should take that to heart.

The national media could have made fun of us. They could have thrown darts at us, the latest target in the American obesity crisis. They could have made jokes about us—*Did you say KFC or OKC?*—or whatever you might see on late-night comedy.

But the story they told was about how a mayor confronted a problem and suggested a solution with humor, energy, and honesty.

After a month or so we held another press conference. We knew of people who had lost a lot of weight so we invited them. I knew we needed a balance of stories, items for the broadcast media as well as for the newspapers.

By this time, the restaurants in town were starting to put low-fat and healthier items on their menus, calling them the Mayor's Special and so on. Some of the top chefs in town put a Mayor's Special salad on the menu every day. Rumor was, wherever the Mayor's Special showed up, it often became the top seller of the day.

There were local Mexican restaurants that were putting a Mayor's Weight Loss Special on the menu, too. That turned out to be an early lesson in how to work with industry to get big things done. We were not going to succeed in combat against the fast-food industry or the private sector in general. I didn't have the money to compete with an industry with marketing and PR dollars and lots of clout. We couldn't win at that game, so I was always hoping to figure out how to get the private sector to support our goals and maybe join in.

Lo and behold, Greg Creed, the CEO of Taco Bell (who later became CEO of all of Yum! Brands), had seen me on *Ellen*. Contrary to what you might think about Taco Bell, the team we worked with was very health conscious inside its corporate community in Southern California. Now, I learned that my appearance on *Ellen* helped drive Taco Bell's decision to be part of America's new attention to obesity.

Sensing there was an opportunity for us to work together, Greg Creed and the Taco Bell team flew into Oklahoma City. As we talked, I mentioned to him another one of those lists I'd seen along the way, where my city was ranked the "Fast-Food Capital of the World." At the time, we had more fast-food restaurants per capita than anywhere else on the planet. Creed's own experience and his company's presence in our city bore that out as well.

Across the metro area, we had forty-five Taco Bells. By comparison, there are about half as many in all five boroughs of New York. Doing the math in my head, I knew that couldn't be good. When I asked how many people in Oklahoma City eat in Taco Bell every day, Creed tapped on his computer for a moment and said, "Thirty-five thousand."

Human Answers to Human Questions

A problem at this scale might be considered a public health emergency. But, I didn't want to take a medical approach. I wanted the solutions we suggested to resemble real life.

How could we expect to change the eating habits of our citizens—those thirty-five thousand people and so many others—that eat fast food every day? This is the food they eat. It's convenient, it seems cheap, or—bottom line—it's just what they want.

I've always considered myself a realist, and I thought one of the problems with traditional diet and obesity information is that it's just not realistic. For decades, we have had doctors and surgeons general putting out messages on the importance of eating five servings of fresh fruits and vegetables daily, and sticking to fish and other low-fat meats. Lots of truth in these messages, but not a lot of relevance to the way most people actually eat.

Maybe one thing I could do is provide a daily dosage of

political incorrectness. Nutritionists and government health experts can't tell people it's okay to go to Taco Bell. But I could.

The only message I wanted to drive home was that people are not defined by their habits. We believed that if there were good choices, and if we promoted them properly, people would choose to eat better. At least they might choose them often enough to make a difference and get an honest conversation started.

So in 2008, we worked with Greg Creed and Taco Bell to roll out and actively promote the "Fresco" side of their menu in Oklahoma City. The Fresco Menu is basically the same menu items, served without sour cream or cheese added, significantly dropping the fat and calories of the meal.

Across the city, Taco Bell put up life-size cardboard cutouts of me at all forty-five of their locations with the slogan across the front, "Because you can't lose a million pounds by yourself."

The popularity of Taco Bell's Fresco Menu was a perfect reminder that eating healthier was about making better choices today, rather than living up to some impossible standard tomorrow.

Recent efforts to enact "soda taxes" in San Francisco, New York, and Philadelphia among others have taken a very different tack, provoking a kind of a mini war between mayors, local governments, and the private sector. Merits of the tax approach aside, my goal was to establish a positive relationship and prove I didn't have any interest in fighting the private sector. We really think it helped set the right tone.

We created an environment where leaders and groups across the spectrum had a reason and a way to work together. To pull on the same rope rather than combatting one another.

Meanwhile, Tom Michaud was having to hire extra people to handle the email traffic that the website was creating.

Thousands of people around the world who had struggled with weight loss wanted to check in on how Oklahoma City was doing, send along advice or good ideas, occasionally sell a product, or just say "Thank you."

When good ideas win a lot of allies across the spectrum, and good work gets positive attention, everyone wants to work harder, together, and make sure the effort turns into impact. And, it turns out that when the mayor puts his city on a diet, the city wants to make sure the mayor is doing his part.

I went to a restaurant soon after the website launched and people were looking to see what I was eating. Then it was all the time. Everybody thought they were the first person to think of this, but I must have heard a million times, "Mayor, is that on your diet?" The entire city was my accountability partner.

My own staff was also engaged and energized. And I am particularly mindful of Tom Michaud and his staff's work. At first, they were just doing their jobs. Over time it became clear that they were all deeply engaged in the mission. The energy was infectious, and it drove us to bigger ideas and greater success.

The business community and the city's largest employers wanted to get on board. We learned quickly that, generally speaking, they weren't the city's problem: Their HR departments are famous for wellness programs and gym memberships and full-package benefits for employees. In the spirit of partnering with rather than picking a fight with employers to achieve a public good, the diet conversation we provoked gave business owners a way to start discussing obesity with their employees for the very first time.

What we did find lacking was the same availability for workers of smaller businesses that didn't have HR departments or budgets to offer wellness benefits to their employees, even though they cared about their employees deeply. Instead, they held meetings to convince their workers and their families to sign up on the website. Responding to demand, we eventually adapted the website for groups to sign up and have the company's pounds lost added up together. Businesses created competitions across departments to see who could lose the most.

Three months into this swell of awareness and work, we had logged over 250,000 pounds lost. We were a quarter of the way there.

It was time for another press conference. We had a great story to celebrate, but we needed another visual to help people understand just how much progress we had made.

I can't remember how, but I eventually figured out that the Air National Guard's KC-135 Stratotankers weighed about 125,000 pounds each. So, there I stood on the tarmac at the Air National Guard headquarters in Oklahoma City, with these two mammoth airplanes showing people just how much weight we had lost. We invited some of the people who had lost the most weight to come and share their success stories. It was an inspiring moment, and a great image. My hope of making progress by simply starting a positive conversation had worked.

For-profit weight-loss groups like Weight Watchers got involved. Business was up for them, and they returned the favor by asking their members to log their progress on a website, thiscityisgoingonadiet.com, as well. Pastors were speaking about obesity from the pulpit. Husbands and wives were connecting over a shared goal to make progress for their own health and the health of their families.

Neighbors would see each other around town and talk about the city's diet—and that infectious energy made all the difference. So many people who had dieted on their own for years and succeeded or failed *now* had a way to make something they wanted to do for themselves a part of something bigger as well.

Over about four years, nearly fifty thousand people signed up on the website, and along with all the participants with our corporate and non-profit partners, our city lost one million pounds. We had done it.

Eventually, my goals for the program were much bigger than just losing those million pounds. It was about raising standards—and raising awareness of how much potential we had in Oklahoma City. With MAPS, we had raised the standards for our quality of life—and thus, our place among America's major metro areas. With the weight-loss initiative, we were doing it again.

We reached the million-pound goal in January 2012, some four years and three weeks after we started. Soon after, I was in New York doing a media tour. I remember I was once again in the waiting room of *Men's Fitness* preparing to talk about some of the work we had done to make our city healthier. While waiting for my interview, I looked down at the coffee table—only to see that year's "fattest cities" list. Somewhat reluctantly, I picked up the magazine to find the story. Where would we be on that list? In the middle? At the end? I at least hoped we were no longer at the top.

Well, we weren't there at all. In fact, the magazine had placed us on the list of fittest cities in America. That's a list worth being on.

A 2017 study of health indicators across the metro area showed improvement in thirteen of fifteen categories—for the first time in a long time. The director of the OKC-County Health Department and the chairman of the board of health agree: Getting people talking honestly is the crucial initial step.

Even more important than our weight loss or our positive media coverage, the million-pound milestone was the foundation of a culture shift in our community that reaches far beyond the choices we make at the dinner table.

What we are building is a generation of Oklahoma City kids who understand that the way they eat affects more than just their waistlines. The choices we make set a course for our success as individuals, our ability to serve others, and our capability to build the city we want to live in. That generation of children will be growing up in a community that looks at health and wellness in a completely different way than any before them.

To make these positive changes in our culture more permanent, we have begun to build our city in dramatically different ways. And in the next chapter, I'll tell you how this idea for putting the city on a diet has allowed us to build our city with our vision set on creating a better future.

LOUISVILLE: BUILDING A CULTURE
OF COMPASSION

Right after I got off the plane in Louisville to meet Mayor Greg Fischer for the first time, it smacked me right in the face: *You're in the 'Ville!*

When it comes to globally recognized brands and institutions that were born in, belong in, and could never leave a city, Louisville suffers from an embarrassment of riches. I knew that Mayor Fischer would have a lot to teach me on this trip, but it was pretty stunning how much I had to learn about building a brand for my city in the middle of Kentucky.

This is the state where bourbon was born, and Louisville has built on that with what Mayor Fischer calls "Bourbonism," the draw when you marry that signature drink and the city's great foodie scene. Louisville is the birthplace of the Greatest of All Time, Muhammad Ali. It's home to the University of Louisville, and of course, the Louisville Slugger.

And then there's the Kentucky Derby. I think y'all know what I mean when I say the Kentucky Derby wouldn't be the Derby if it was held anywhere else.

For one day each year—the first Saturday in May—the eyes of the world turn to Louisville. And thousands travel there, racking up tremendous value for the city in the form of hotel rooms, rental cars, and elaborate dinners out. But from the city's perspective, the Derby's true value is immeasurable.

So right here, right now, I'm naming Louisville, Kentucky, the #1 Best-Branded City in the World.

But Louisville is also a pretty innovative place—and it's one of those cities where innovation has been led by local government.

In the early 2000s, former mayor Jerry Abramson led a charge to unify the city and county governments, which led to huge increases in the government's productivity taxpayer savings. Overnight, Louisville jumped from the sixty-fifth to the eighteenth largest city in the country. The citizens liked the new Louisville Metro government so much they made Abramson take the job for a second time.

And under the leadership of Mayor Fischer, an innovative entrepreneur who just happens to be mayor, that legacy of government-led innovation is booming in the 'Ville, with the city undertaking some of the coolest tech-driven developments through their Office of Civic Innovation. For example, they've started working on something that few of us talk about much in daily conversation but will soon be common dinner-table talk: the Internet of Things—a nickname for the changes we will experience when not just our phones, but our fridges, cars, buses, and buildings all share data in real time.

When you equip everyday objects with Internet connections, a simple children's asthma inhaler becomes an incredible digital tool. In Louisville, these Internet-enhanced inhalers don't just help doctors provide better real-time care to kids, but also feed the city data on air quality, allowing decision makers to identify pollution hotspots and craft health policy with an eye toward prediction rather than reacting after the damage is done.

Underneath these kinds of tech-driven projects lies a deeper question of the city's culture: What values make it such an innovative place?

When I started the whole diet idea, I was mostly thinking about the city's health. But the crucial thing beneath that was working within our city to raise standards and build a culture devoted to positive change.

Louisville mayor Greg Fischer thinks about culture, too, and in some really powerful and surprising ways.

Like most mayors, he feels that his city's brand is crucial to his plans for securing the city's place in the twenty-first-century economy. And most other mayors would kill for the constellation of brands and institutions Louisville has, so you'd expect the city to market its existing attractions and events, luring visitors to sell more hotel rooms at home and more bourbon around the world. But there's something deeper and more important in a brand and a city than just the dollars and cents.

In 2016, I asked Mayor Fischer to come to Oklahoma City and speak to me and my neighbors about his initiative to build a compassionate city, focused on helping individuals build their own practices of prayer, mindfulness, and meditation, and encouraging the city as a whole to become a community that responds with kindness and compassion when troubles arise.

Mayor Fischer has an interesting way of talking about it. He thinks of the compassion work he encourages as building "social muscle." When bad times come—a company closes or a terrible crime occurs—it's helpful to have "banked" compassion and goodwill among the people.

I'm reminded of a detail about Oklahoma City's experience in the moments after the bombing, when we learned that many residents who were nearby instinctively ran toward the danger, and not away. People lucky enough to be unharmed worked side by side with first responders to pull others from the rubble. The story also goes that the money blown out of a vault in the building's bank was eventually all accounted for. That morning, Oklahoma City had some banked compassion to draw on.

Probably, most people in most American cities would do the same. It's a remarkable feature of our country's ethic that we must appreciate as a unique strength for such a large society.

What is so remarkable about Louisville and Mayor Fischer's work, however, is the proactive attempt to build that social muscle and make that moral strength more and more powerful. And he swings for the fences.

In 2013, as part of the mayor's work to earn a global distinction as a compassionate city, Louisville was lucky enough to have scheduled a visit from the Dalai Lama. When it comes to bringing fame to your city, there are only one or two names that might be bigger than that.

When the Dalai Lama was in Louisville, the mayor helped stage arena-scale events at the local KFC Yum! Center for citizens and students. And rather than host some high-dollar fund-raiser for CEOs and developers across the metro area, Mayor Fischer also put together a quiet, private meeting between His Holiness and the city's senior managers. In a move I imagine produced serious fretting and furrowing of brows, he also suggested to his staff that each of them ask the Dalai Lama a question related to their department's daily work.

This practice is bearing real fruit. Mayor Fischer's team focused on attracting companies and building jobs—but first, they thought carefully and creatively about the kinds of companies they wanted to attract. They help new and existing companies understand that the biggest drags on productivity in the workplace come from poor workplace culture and unnecessary conflict among team members.

At the social level, the work to "bank compassion" seems to be paying off, too. Returning to those high-tech asthma inhalers, the project was inspired by the frame of mind that such a difficult health problem could be solved only in an environment where parents and families were directly engaged with the change.

No agency or bureaucracy could hope to crack the code.

Entrenched problems need new kinds of solutions. By adding compassion to his city's toolkit, Mayor Greg Fischer has done something truly special that anyone and any place can replicate.

And knowing that improving your child's health could help your neighbors stay well, too? That is the kind of "brand experience" every city should strive to provide.

CHAPTER 8

Building for the Future

B eing a sportscaster is a surprisingly unathletic profession. Over the first two decades of my adulthood, my schedule was unpredictable at best and totally chaotic at worst. Despite the fact that the athletes I was writing about and talking to were in top physical condition, my life was mostly spent in a seated position. Sitting in a press box, sitting on a stool in front of the camera, or very frequently sitting in my car.

Often, my daily routine started around three-thirty a.m. and took me from my driveway in the suburbs to my parking spot at the TV station. After some long hours in windowless, soundproof rooms, I would reverse my steps, fly along the highway, and park the car right back in the garage. Back home at night, I'd often end up sitting for hours in front of the television instead of behind the camera. On my days off, if I told my sons we were running an errand around the block, the first thing they would do is go hunting for my keys. Days like that, I probably spent a total of less than two minutes outdoors.

This was far from a problem for just my family or my neighborhood. Across Oklahoma City, we had neglected our sidewalks and streets for decades. Our parks were well-mowed lawns, but offered almost nothing for kids and families to do. Thanks to the isolation we enjoyed in our cars, we often joked that we didn't even know our next-door neighbors' names. Without our bothering to notice, our neighborhoods and the people that lived in them were becoming increasingly isolated from one another as well.

By the time I became mayor in 2004, the city had come a long way. Through MAPS and its second iteration, MAPS for Kids, we were building world-class amenities, arenas, and schools that would attract people and jobs to downtown Oklahoma City for the first time in decades. The city looked great on TV. There was water in the river, for Pete's sake! We won more than our share of economic development awards and occasionally would be mentioned in the national media as an up-and-coming place. From the ashes, we were becoming a city that could attract sporting events; tourists; talented, educated workers; and the jobs that would follow them.

But something important was still missing.

After we started talking about obesity and began losing weight in 2008, I knew the conversation needed to expand. The way our city was built was outdated. We had allowed urban sprawl to dominate our planning perspectives. I began to understand the importance of a city's design and how it affected the health of its citizens.

An Incredible Quality of Life (for Our Cars)

It might have taken a lot longer than it should have, but eventually we saw the problem for what it was. Our entire city was built around the automobile. Oklahoma City was an incredible place to live . . . if you were a car.

But if you happened to be a *person,* you were seemingly combatting cars at every turn.

Our downtown was almost totally one-way streets. Many of them were five lanes wide. Traffic flowed really well. I suppose this was a good idea if your entire goal was to see how fast you could move people to the interstate on-ramp and out of downtown.

But through the MAPS projects and private development we had spent well over a billion dollars downtown trying to get people to stay.

If we wanted to make our downtown more than a place to visit by car, leaving the streets and walkways the way they were was a nonstarter. Just try crossing those five-lane downtown thoroughfares on foot. When anyone hit the "Walk" button at an intersection, "Don't Walk" started flashing in just about three seconds. The message to pedestrians was less "Don't Walk" than "GET OUT OF THE WAY!"

Once I realized this basic problem, I saw it everywhere I looked. Our schools and offices and even our churches were designed around the convenience of our cars. When a new building was built, the closest thing to the street was the parking lot. Then the car drop-off, then the building itself. The idea that transportation might include other modes like walking or biking seemed to be the furthest thing from our minds.

The fast-food industry might have pioneered the "drive-thru" concept, but it felt like we were intent on building a drive-thru city from the ground up, too.

To make it official, we had zoned our city as if everyone owned a car and drove everywhere they went. For example, if you wanted to build an office or a store or a movie theater, the city would mandate parking that gobbled up valuable urban spaces.

The problem extended far beyond our downtown and road-ways, too. Because nobody was really visiting them to notice, our parks had been underfunded and had fallen into disrepair. We passed a bond issue for parks in 1975 but didn't pass another until 1995. We were hopelessly behind. We rarely bothered to connect anything by sidewalk, and for several decades didn't re-quire developers to construct them in residential neighborhoods.

When I was elected mayor, there were thousands of homes and entire neighborhoods in our community with literally no sidewalks in sight. Out in those suburban neighborhoods, it wasn't just the huge number of fast-food chains that I started noticing.

As I began to understand how a city's health can be influ-enced by the built environment, I started thinking critically about what it meant to build a city in which people wanted to grow a business, raise their families, and make their lives. Like many cities across the country, we had responded naturally to the incentives created by federal tax and development policy. For a couple of generations, we had never really looked at downtown or the city's neighborhoods as places you'd want to spend any time. It was almost like our roads and bridges and the city as a whole were built with an escape route in mind.

The Advantage of Desperation

Desperate times call for desperate measures. The economic collapse of the 1980s had taken a physical and emotional toll. Our citizens knew the city was falling behind and the deferred maintenance in our infrastructure, parks, and schools piled up quickly. And there was as little hope then as there is now that a long-term solution would be forthcoming from the state-house or Washington, D.C.

It's much easier to motivate people to use tax dollars for change if they understand there's a problem. We were in a really bad place. They understood. So, as a city seeking to better itself, we had benefited from what I call "the advantage of desperation."

In this new mission to change how our city was built, desperation was not something I could rely on. Our streets were just the way they were, and nobody seemed to notice it at all. The foundations of our auto-centered city had been laid long before the invention of the automobile.

Back to the 1889 Oklahoma Land Run, our downtown, and therefore the city as a whole, had been laid out with really, really wide streets. It made good enough sense then: The horse and buggy needed plenty of room to make incredibly wide turns.

As Oklahoma City grew and the economy changed, there was never an urgent enough reason to spend millions to narrow the streets or even question why things were built the way they were. The out-migration from our downtown to cheaper, more spacious suburbs compounded its effect, and over time the cycle of plummeting property values and declining investment accelerated. If people wanted something different, there was always room to build out in the countryside or the suburbs—and plenty of potential new customers.

But the need for change was even more urgent than it appeared. Our health and weight had suffered in part because of this auto-dependent culture. Beyond that, we had just about the most unfriendly and dangerous environment a pedestrian could encounter. Across our city, kids and families, especially those families who could not afford a car, were forced to walk or bike alongside cars in the middle of busy streets.

In 2008, right about the same time as the city's diet got us looking at our city with new eyes, that urgency made itself known in the national media.

Prevention magazine and the American Podiatric Medical Association released a list of America's most walkable cities. It was an exhaustive study, with over eighteen thousand data points from five hundred markets across every state in the union. While the article wasn't purely scientific, this was one of the rare lists that actually meant something. With these new questions on my mind, the article taught me a lot.

For fun I guess, they included the *least walkable* cities in America as well.

And there we were. Dead last, 500 out of 500.

That's an embarrassing place to be. And there's not much a city staff can do. Dig up all the streets? Expanding a single sidewalk or redesigning a single block would cost millions of dollars. And there are always other demands for our precious tax dollars.

It's difficult to solve a problem if you don't know the problem exists. Most people were ready to just enjoy our success for a while. Our city and downtown were so much better than anyone could remember. Our streets don't need any work! When was the last time you got caught in a traffic jam?

Others wanted to stay focused on what we knew was working. Our MAPS initiatives and other work were focused on ambitious, headline-grabbing, job-creating projects. Why should we spend money on something as dull as sidewalks, bike paths, and trails?

Others still were ready to give all this progress a rest. In deep red Oklahoma, it wasn't hard to predict that support for more taxes, however they'd be spent, would be an uphill climb. Hadn't we spent enough money? Hadn't we made Oklahoma City good enough already?

I didn't want us to be just good enough. We were trying to become a world-class city, not just measure up to our peers in the region.

With the diet under our belts and honest conversations about our health under way, I thought it was a good moment to tap into people's renewed interest in health and wellness across our city.

Good to Great: Connecting Our Successes

Back in 2002, when I was new on the city council, I attended a presentation by our parks director on the Oklahoma City Trails Master Plan. The plan was beautiful and comprehensive enough to win a series of federal grants, and we annually would build a few more miles. But this exhaustive plan was embarrassingly underbuilt.

I didn't understand. I raised my hand and asked what I thought sounded like a pretty reasonable question. Federal grants are great and all but at the rate we were going . . . What was the plan to pay for the rest of the seventy miles of trails?

First, there was a snicker or two from the back of the room. Followed by an awkward silence. Then outright laughter.

The joke was on me. There was no funding plan for the Master Plan. No public budget. Absolutely none. Though there was some private funding in place for some of the more scenic parts of the plan, you actually had to drive to get to them. By the time that grand network of trails would be built, all of us sitting in that room would be dead and gone.

By 2008, a lot had changed. There was our downtown turn-around, and our diet and wellness experience to build on. I sensed a deeper change as well. The millennials and young professionals that were finally moving to our city were now ready to invest in the walkability and wellness projects that our city's developers and urban planners had dreamt up a decade before. With the third vote for the MAPS sales tax on the horizon, we sensed the opportunity to make that Master Plan a reality.

The city's MAPS 3 website was attracting a lot of attention and good ideas. About two thousand suggestions came pouring into the site in just a couple of months.

Once the initial set of ideas came in, we narrowed down to those that had support from city leadership and turned to some more scientific polling to see what the voting public would really support on the ballot.

The chamber of commerce and business community were unsurprisingly pushing for a new convention center, which was badly needed and had been on the wish list at least as long as I'd been mayor. We had worked with the federal government and our representatives in Congress to move a section of Interstate 40 several blocks south of downtown, creating an opportunity to use MAPS to build a new public green space of seventy acres or more. We were inspired by a visit to Charlotte's waterfront to build a kayaking facility to complement the rowing projects that Mike Knopp and his colleagues had launched.

Some other projects were on the list for consideration. A new investment in the city's tennis center, or the infrastructure needed to bring an IndyCar Grand Prix downtown. Projects like these have a small but vocal audience. They didn't poll well. People didn't want to include them in MAPS 3.

What surprised me was how people were reacting to trails

and sidewalks in the polls. Our instincts were right. Health was resonating. Despite the opinions of many that MAPS support would focus on more large-scale projects with a clear economic development impact, investments in connecting our city were polling a few points higher than any of those "major" projects were.

A majority of our citizens had come to believe that part of the next step, moving the city from a good place to a great city, would depend on our ability to connect. To connect our neighborhoods and our downtown. Connect the projects we had built to each other. And to connect our people to the city they call home. More and more people were beginning to understand that transportation should include walking and riding a bike. They were ready to invest in physical fitness.

Like MAPS and MAPS for Kids, MAPS 3 was a package of items combined into one initiative. As I was visiting with the business community and the city council to put the list together in the summer of 2009, each of the items polled over 50 percent. The election was called for December.

In the end, the MAPS 3 package passed by a 54–46 margin. What we came to understand was that sidewalks and bike paths and a downtown streetcar system were not just for show, or nice things to have. A connected city is an economically strong city. Big buildings and flashy projects may give us places to go—but connections like sidewalks, trails, and transit give us better ways to get there.

The Ultimate Corporate Citizen

The night MAPS 3 passed, there was a pretty good party in the city's Cox Convention Center. Once we were really sure, I took the stage alongside the city council and announced, "The votes are in, and Oklahoma City's Golden Age continues." Not everyone in the city was happy about it that night; our campaign to pass MAPS 3 had actually drawn funded opposition. But I was certain we would all work to make sure those projects met or exceeded the voters' expectations.

As all this was taking place, we were in the early stages of executing a public-private partnership that would integrate well with the MAPS 3 projects. The state's largest business, Devon Energy, was constructing a new headquarters and worked with us to create a huge makeover of our downtown streets and parks.

Maybe New Yorkers and Angelenos and Chicagoans won't understand this, but when your city gets a new skyscraper out in Middle America, it's a pretty big deal. Quite beyond the $750 million the company would be investing into a single city block, the image of your city on national newscasts literally rises to a whole new level. For the first time in thirty years, the skyline would get a major addition.

This level of investment also makes a mayor feel proud—in a time when energy companies were growing in Dallas, Houston, and other global cities, Devon was making it clear they were here to stay. In truth, we would have done almost anything to keep them if they had threatened to leave.

But rather than try to extort the city for an aggressive tax break or to force our hand on some city council vote, you can imagine our delight when Devon's CEO called with a very different idea in mind.

Devon was led by co-founder Larry Nichols, and he knew that beyond what the building's construction would do to boost local business in the short-term, the long-term impact on property values and property taxes would be substantial. Larry called because he had an unusually ambitious idea about how to put that future value to use right away.

So, there's this pretty interesting borrowing tool that cities use all the time in circumstances like these. Interesting as the tool is, it has a pretty boring name.

Here's how "tax increment financing" (TIF) usually works: When a city or county has the prospect of a large new development project bringing investment and development to an area, the future taxes generated by that new investment can be captured by the city or county for the purposes of financing infrastructure required for that same new development. So for a period of years, a piece of the neighborhood's property tax is redirected to such a special project that helps a neighborhood or a project's development along. The government can borrow money secured by the increased tax revenue to fund the needed infrastructure. Make sense?

The problem with TIFs is time. It takes time for buildings to go up and even more time for the property taxes to actually increase. These projects can take forever, and forever was an amount of time that Devon felt they didn't have.

The whole point of investing in growing their company downtown was to attract the best new hires they could and to potentially attract other corporate headquarters to downtown. More and more millennial workers and top talent no longer wanted to live or work in the sprawling suburbs, but preferred a more accessible, walkable environment. Telling a recent graduate from a top-flight MBA program that downtown would be terrific in four to seven years? Not so much.

Rather than going out to lenders to back a plan for a walkable, active downtown before their building was really under way, Devon took an incredible step and financed the project to the city themselves. And rather than focus the projects they would fund right around their property, leaving the rest of downtown to the city or other companies in the area, they wanted to fund a revamp of over fifty downtown blocks.

It is important to take this all in: A giant oil and gas company, with demanding investors inspecting every line of their balance sheet, invested in improving the streetscape and walkability for their city. Playing against type, an oil and gas company was actively financing a departure from our decades-long romance with the automobile. In Devon Energy and Chairman Nichols, we had found the pinnacle of corporate citizenship.

On our own, the city council and Public Works departments had put together plans for some modest, incremental downtown improvements, but the TIF financing from the Devon tower would allow us to really think big.

A 180-Degree Turnaround in Two Years and on 180 Acres

I hate clichés, but this one sort of made sense. We wanted to continue our city's dramatic turnaround among our downtown streets. With Devon's support, we were able to work toward a total turnaround of 180 acres of our city: Project 180. The name stuck.

I had already been working on a plan to get people walking downtown and had convinced the city to hire the nationally recognized city planner and urban mobility innovator Jeff Speck, whom I had met at a mayor's planning conference several years earlier.

Jeff's job in our city and many others is to ask really big questions and get us to set higher standards for ourselves. He pushed exactly the buttons I wanted him to push. In his initial research for the city, Speck made some radical suggestions.

Take all your five-lane roads and make them into two lanes of moving traffic. Narrow those two lanes down by several feet. Then add a bicycle lane, or add a couple lanes of parking.

Take all those one-way "evacuation routes" built to get people in and out of downtown as fast as possible, and make them two-way streets with a lot more streetlights.

Turning lanes? Get rid of all your right-hand lanes and limit left-turn lanes to places where a lot of people actually turn left. We don't have any more horse-and-buggy traffic to worry about.

And overall, cut your streets' vehicle and traffic capacity in half, since it was twice what we apparently needed.

These might not seem like terrible ideas to people who love, or live, downtown. But there was a collision of minds awaiting. We had civil engineers who knew we couldn't spend all this money to create gridlock. And they were every bit as committed to their cause as Speck.

What came first was a "professional review" of Speck's suggestions by the city's teams and a group of our traditional engineering consultants that put the new approach to downtown's streets and traffic through the old-school, car-centric computer models that the city had used for decades. All of Jeff's ideas about narrower lanes, two-way streets, storefront parking, and spaces for bikes and strollers and people were put to the test against the crush of daily traffic. Predictably, the calculations of the old-school models foretold a future just short of an apocalypse.

But Speck's approach took a fresh look at how our new residents and next-generation businesses actually used our streets. This new way of looking at things told us pretty plainly that we had more lanes than our demand for traffic really required. There was plenty of evidence a two-lane street could handle ten thousand cars a day—and our five-lane thoroughfares were only moving nine thousand cars a day. The space to make the change happen was there.

But because our city was built around the automobile, I was really afraid that making even modest changes downtown could be the hardest project of all. At dozens of conferences on urban innovation over the years, I'd heard the gospel of walkability from some of the brightest city thinkers on earth. What they said about bike lanes, millennials' car-free lifestyle, and the coming impact of driverless automobiles all rang true. But disrupting traffic downtown went straight to the heart of our car-first culture.

Even before taking on downtown businesses or changing workers' commutes, convincing our city planners and civil engineers promised to be a major battlefield. Essentially I was asking them to measure their success differently from how they had their entire careers. This was going to be the fight of my life.

Or so I thought.

It definitely wasn't easy at first, but it turned out that our city's engineering and traffic professionals became some of our greatest advocates, basically overnight. This should really have been no surprise: Our planners have been working on cities their entire professional lives! They didn't need to be convinced as much as they needed permission to think and act creatively.

With some compromises, coping with unsuspected budget cuts, and a lot of hard work, we adapted the plans and launched into what felt like the most ambitious work we'd ever done in Oklahoma City. For those of us not immediately familiar with the size of an acre, the space we ended up transforming is equivalent to more than 130 football fields.

According to Speck, no other city in the United States has redesigned all of its downtown streets or updated them all at once the way we did. Even our planning director at the time, Russell Claus, said, "This is one of those twenty-year overnight success stories."

Laura Story, the city's own civil engineer, said:

> My experience with respect to designing and building this urban downtown street system involved changing my perspective, questioning the standard typical sections for streets, and realizing there are many users of urban streets—personal vehicles, delivery vehicles, buses, refuse collection, pedestrians, able-bodied and disabled people, and cyclists. The city has exploded with new recreation, entertainment, and eating venues. The demographics of our city have changed so much with the influx of young adults starting their careers; downtown feels alive and metropolitan. The neighborhood of downtown has a new, fresh, and well-kept front yard—what urban-loving individual wouldn't enjoy this new feeling?

This whole experience was definitely like drinking out of a fire hose. I would later joke that we called it Project 180 because it seemed like we were trying to do 180 things all at once. On top of the skyscraper construction, and the finishing work to ready Chesapeake Energy Arena as the Thunder's new home, we had a tremendous number of our downtown streets under construction to support all this growth. It would be a big black eye if all this work didn't run smoothly.

On the front lines was our city manager, Jim Couch. A civil engineer himself, he brilliantly walked the tightrope of traffic flow versus walkability and beautification. We were building a city for the future. A city we knew we could enjoy and that our children would fondly remember growing up in. One that was well connected and highly regarded by journalists and designers, and not forgetting the companies and entrepreneurs we wanted to be a part of our city and our community for generations to come.

Sure, we had some unusual circumstances in our overall momentum, and a strong economy. Our corporate partner in Devon Energy provided a financing source that would have been very hard to duplicate anywhere else at that time. But that was then, and this is now, and what we did is possible in your city, too.

The most impactful changes we made to boost our downtown's walkability took a lot more work than they did capital. Narrower lanes, angled parking, and safe spaces for bikers and pedestrians need two things: paint and a willing public.

For his own part, Jeff Speck told an audience of three hundred and fifty mayors at the U.S. Conference of Mayors national meeting that our work together was the most impressive he had ever seen or been involved with. As he said so many times, and as I hope he tells many of your mayors and engineers and neighbors, "The battle for a walkable city is mostly between the curbs."

Those battles signal a deeper cultural shift in our residents and our city's leadership, too. By changing what we thought was possible in our streets and blocks, we opened the door to much bigger actions in how our streets and sidewalks, transit and trails, parks and schools and trees fit together to become a city that is truly built for the future.

CHATTANOOGA: INVESTING IN PEOPLE—
EVERY CITY'S GREATEST ASSET

In our last story, from Louisville, we might have decided that the 'Ville is the best-branded city in the country. But there's little question that the city with the best nicknames in the nation is Chattanooga. And their ongoing story of urban revitalization—and their efforts to ensure that the benefits of change reach across neighborhoods and beyond racial, economic, and cultural barriers—is one to behold.

Just over thirty years ago, around the same time Oklahoma City was in the depths of despair, Chattanooga was beginning to put those principles into practice. The ideas that drove their positive change then and continue to do so now might sound familiar today, but in those days the city leaders' guiding insight was truly groundbreaking. What did those leaders do that was so different? They listened.

Hearing the Headlines, Enlisting Unusual Leaders

Chattanooga was founded as a trading post on the banks of a gentle bend in the Tennessee River in 1815, and its growth accelerated just two decades later when its geography and beauty drew thousands to the end of the Western and Atlantic Railroad. The city's unique position at the intersection of major trade routes, its strong infrastructure, and its stunning natural beauty gave it its first nicknames.

At different times in its history, Chattanooga has been declared the "Gateway to the South" and—sorry, Paris—the "City of Lights." Some folks who are into the whole brevity thing call it "Chatt," while others opt for "Nooga." Take your pick.

At the height of its industrial and manufacturing power, the city became known as the "Dynamo of Dixie." The river's power and access to markets made it a natural home for growth across the industrial revolution as well as the post-war manufacturing boom in the twentieth century. As we've learned, though, too much of a good thing in one place can sometimes be a problem.

Now, Noogans have heard this story a thousand times, so I'll keep it short. The river valley's beauty became a trap when the factories were full of workers, smokestacks steamed day and night, and tailpipes spewed exhaust into the air. Like the air pollution hotspots back in Louisville, the valley that rings Chattanooga captured the pollution—and the air got bad.

Really bad. In the 1960s, Chattanooga's businessmen routinely brought two shirts to work with them: one white shirt for the morning, and an afternoon shirt for when soot turned their white collars gray. Local drivers had trouble, too: The soot lingering in the river valley air was bad enough that drivers in the City of Lights were forced to drive with their headlamps on all day. Pollution in Chattanooga was bad enough that tourists to "Scenic City" reportedly complained to hotel managers that the dust settling overnight was stripping the paint from their cars.

At that time, Chattanooga was far from alone in its struggle with pollution and environmental damage. I remember in the years before President Richard Nixon began building the Environmental Protection Agency, you could see with your own eyes how much pollution our enormous cars were putting into the air. Across Oklahoma's plains, though, the wind blows the pollution away almost immediately. We were probably contributing as much or more to the problem, but we didn't see the effects on anything close to the scale that Chattanooga witnessed.

In 1969, just a few months after the polluted Cuyahoga River had caught fire in Cleveland, the still-forming EPA released a study detailing the depths of America's environmental crisis. In what seems to be the prototypical "List of Cities," Walter Cronkite announced to the nation on the CBS *Evening News* a new, not-so-scenic nickname for the City of Lights.

According to Uncle Walter and the EPA, Chattanooga was the "Dirtiest City in America."

With an urgency that reminds me of Mayor Norick's actions after United Airlines announced its move to Indianapolis, Chattanooga took action. In truth, the writing had been on the wall for some time, so there was ample political will to get local policies changed and begin enforcement of higher air- and water-quality standards. The federal government and its nascent EPA pitched in some grant funds to get them pointed in the right direction, too. But the situation was bad, far beyond what a few small government grants could handle.

Chattanooga's tourism industry wasn't exactly the backbone of the local economy, but it was very important. And tourists are finicky and fickle, so with the "Dirtiest City" moniker hanging in the air, the city couldn't wait for federal support to arrive. Within months, governments across the region created a new air quality commission to tackle the problem head-on.

At the head of that change was Dr. Marion Barnes, president of the Christian school Covenant College in nearby Lookout Mountain, Georgia, which had just moved to the region a few years earlier. Now, that might not seem obvious: looking to a newly arrived religious leader from a neighboring state to lead an environmental cleanup initiative driven by some pretty complex science. But Dr. Barnes was also a Columbia

University–trained chemist. And from high atop Lookout Mountain, he could clearly see the impact of local pollution every day. In fact, the air was so bad the smog came in through cracks in the windows in the retrofitted resort hotel that Covenant College called home in those days.

Long story short, the commission headed by Dr. Barnes was able to lead industry changes and cleanup projects that dramatically increased air quality in the city and around the region. Relying mostly on the power of persuasion, Chattanooga cleaned up its air within the three-year timeframe it had set as a goal.

Listening to the River and to Each Other

Maybe it was the way the community pulled together to reclaim its Scenic City status. Maybe it was how a group of established leaders got big ideas in their heads, or how a group of new leaders wound up in Chattanooga around the same time. Maybe it was just the rush of fresh air from the cleanup. But something in Chattanooga in the late 1970s launched one of the biggest urban transformations in our nation's history.

At that time, downtown Chattanooga was just like most other American downtowns—losing jobs by the hundreds and companies by the dozens to suburban office parks. Residents followed, leaving those workers and residents that remained feeling isolated and unsafe. There is a downward spiral in property value and investment as you can imagine, but the spiral affects many things more important than property values. The decay from a dead downtown ultimately seeps into the soul of a city.

Chattanooga had long been a capital of entrepreneurship and industrious workers. That meant it also became home to some powerful and generous philanthropists. In antebellum times, men would find their way to Chattanooga and set their hands to ambitious projects. One of those people was named John Lupton. And while Coca-Cola was invented in Atlanta, it was first bottled in Chattanooga, making the Luptons and a number of other families pretty darn wealthy.

Like a lot of fabulously rich people, the Lupton family was generous with their giving, but they gave in fairly traditional ways—to hospitals and universities and local non-profits and so forth. That was until 1977, when John Lupton's son, Cartter, died and left control of the company and the philanthropies to his son Jack. Jack Lupton evidently saw that a city that retreated to the suburbs and nearby mountainsides risked not being a city at all. In today's lingo, Jack Lupton and his son-in-law Rick Montague deployed a campaign of disruptive innovation in the family's giving. And their disruptive approach centered on listening.

At the time, there was a very different, expert-driven approach to zoning, city planning, and community development. Imagine for a moment what middle managers at IBM or General Motors would have designed for a city in the mid-1970s, and you'll get a sense of what city planning was like. No wonder so much development was happening in the suburbs: Top-down principles work only when you're starting up from scratch.

The Lupton family's Lyndhurst Foundation, on the other hand, started listening to see what other places might be doing, to learn what they had missed. To figure out what the cities that had hit their stride five or ten years earlier had done to achieve it. Austin might not have been happening just yet, but lots of other places featured in these pages were. Indianapolis and Seattle were on the rise under Mayors Hudnut and Royer. Taking note of that, Rick Montague traveled the country and brought inventive ideas and people back with him.

Listening to other cities helped, but what made the biggest difference was listening to the people of Chattanooga about what their own city needed. The first listening effort was called the Moccasin Bend Task Force, named for a piece of neglected land at a bend in the Tennessee River where the Chatt had started up from nothing two centuries before. The ideas the community members generated not only created ideas for turning that liability into an asset for the city, but also unearthed deeper problems that the city would need to solve. After that, the germ of a program called "Chattanooga Venture" sprouted up, and Eleanor Cooper and many others continued the process that Lupton, Montague, and the Lyndhurst Foundation had sparked.

In the mayors' club, you might hear this practice called the "Chattanooga Way"—a term I gather was coined by one of the city's better-known former mayors, Senator Bob Corker. Lots of cities have a name for their special culture or particular way of getting things done. Listening commissions and community vision boards are pretty commonplace now, too. But at the time, the extent to which local leaders faithfully followed real input from the people was pretty radical. The folks who created the Chattanooga Way had no certainty about where they were going. But I think they knew they were headed the right way.

Losing Direction and Finding It Again

This is not to say the Chattanooga Way was always smooth. In the midst of the process, then governor Lamar Alexander was looking to make his mark on the state. He could sense the energy building in Chattanooga and knew that the Luptons and other donors had deep pockets. On a sizable piece of property along the otherwise-neglected Tennessee River, Governor Alexander and Jack Lupton advanced a plan for a major regional attraction. It would create jobs, revitalize undervalued property, spur private investment, invite thousands of money-spending tourists, and all the rest of the things that people say about megaprojects.

Looking back, I don't think too many people would want to erase the Tennessee Aquarium from the Chattanooga skyline, but throughout the 1970s and 1980s, there were real conversations about whether that was the *best thing* to do with that land and money. Some members of the community disagreed with the project at the time and felt that other concerns simply weren't being heard. On grounds of economic development and community growth, the aquarium was the first visible sign of rebirth in Chattanooga, which was followed by an overall revitalization of the riverfront, a reinvention of the city's downtown, and the public sector's leadership in building the nation's first citywide gigabit-per-second fiber network.

Decades later, the issues of equity in opportunity and income, as well as lingering issues of race and class, are rising again in new and important ways. On the one hand, many of these pressing issues might not have received the attention they deserved in the beginning stages. But on the other, the people of Chattanooga certainly seem to be in a better position to have those conversations now than they were before the city's renaissance began.

The city's current leadership does seem intent on making a meaningful pivot now that a strong foundation rests under their feet. There are plenty of new programs and ideas to mention, but the most encouraging thing I've heard is that Mayor Andy Berke and other city leaders are thinking about development from an entirely different perspective. In the same way that we started building Oklahoma City from the perspective of people rather than cars, Chattanooga's development concepts seem trained to invest primarily in people, rather than simply building new, gleaming buildings and projects. In Oklahoma City, we learned that investing in ourselves means investing in our children. Through a variety of tools and big ideas, Chattanooga is poising itself to be a leader also in early-childhood development and education.

The shift might be thought of this way: Chattanooga is moving from a strategy of placemaking to one of "peoplemaking." In an era when talent drives growth and jobs move to people, this is building a city for the future on a new level.

The Lessons We Can All Learn

I hope as you read along in this story you noticed just how many other moments and ideas from other chapters in this book resonated. Maybe you noticed some I didn't mention at all. See, I don't think this is merely a coincidence. The cities we are studying have as much in common as they have things that make them distinct. But it's not just that we're in the same boat, either.

The more I learn about Chattanooga—and the others that flourished a generation earlier than mine—the more hopefully I look to the future in Oklahoma City. The problems we have faced and the things we've accomplished in the past ten years feel quite similar to what Chattanooga and Boston, Seattle and Portland, Charlotte and Atlanta, Austin and Nashville faced fifteen and twenty years ago.

What I mean is that we in Oklahoma City would be fortunate to work through the hard issues as well as Chattanooga and other cities in that elite group of revitalized places like Austin, Boston, Seattle, Nashville, and more. And as our cities grow and change, we should learn common lessons and find ways to apply their wisdom and insights in our own context and our own time.

The narrative in Chattanooga follows quite closely what we have learned from other cities in these pages, too. The revitalized riverfront attracted immense investments downtown backed by some unusual advocates in the broader metro region. This is quite a dramatic turnaround, from being named the dirtiest city in America to being named the "Best Town Ever" by *Outside* magazine in 2015.

Like other cities in our story, Chattanooga identified critical leadership from unusual places, such as Dr. Marion Barnes's contributions to the environment from his seat as a leader of a Christian college atop nearby Lookout Mountain. And Jack Lupton's investment of time and money in his city, which was made possible largely as a consequence of his big idea for Coca-Cola that failed miserably in the middle of 1985. That's right— New Coke was Jack Lupton's pet project. Luckily for all of us, he had better ideas for reinventing his hometown.

I could go on. Echoes of the other stories in this book are there to be found—with Chattanooga and with many other places I'm certain. The issues Chattanooga is wrestling with today are likely on the horizon for the rest of the next hundred Austins I hope our country builds. As they work together, we will be watching and learning. And if they stumble, I hope they ask for help yet again. I know my city will be ready to lend a hand. Perhaps yours will be, too.

CHAPTER 9

Punching Above Our Weight

One of my favorite things is driving across what most people call "rural America." Away from the interstates. Far from the big cities. But still in many ways the heart of the story of our country's urbanization.

When we have the chance to get away, my wife and I love to venture into the small hamlets that once served as the country's thriving centers of business and community. The places that sprouted up the last time our nation's cities grew the way they are growing today. Many of them are struggling and emptying out. Many others, however, are flourishing, and you're about to see why.

Sometimes you have to use your imagination to see what was. In the eastern half of the United States these towns are full of sturdy, beautiful century-old buildings that might have once housed a factory or a bank or a drugstore. But now, the signs indicate the last business to bother giving it a try was a flea market. And your eye tells you that even that was at least a few years back.

Your mind reverts to the pre-flea-market days when these towns thrived. Originally, they may have grown from a railroad junction or a trading post situated along a twist in a river. You can picture a happier time. No one comes along now to erase them from the landscape, so many of these towns wither and decay, one season, one year at a time. How did this happen?

A generation ago, there were good jobs here. Sometimes manufacturing. Sometimes agriculture. Each town might have multiple banks and schools and churches.

But along the way, the good times ended. Small farms couldn't compete with big farms. Jobs were growing in the bigger cities. Kids went away to college and didn't come back.

We do know one explanation: The interstate highway system, designed for defense as much as trade, connected our main cities and strategic assets to each other. Hundreds of cities along those corridors have thrived. But thousands and thousands of smaller towns connected by country roads and county highways have withered. Most of these places have become dots on a map. They are not well known. They might be places where people are from, but they don't strike you as places people will end up.

Some of these towns were located close enough to urban centers that they were gobbled up by developers and annexed over time. And though they were originally not along the interstate corridors, they were eventually connected by expanded city highways and interstate loops. Many of those towns became the suburbs and have their own unique stories. They invested in schools and took advantage of their geography. Eventually, if not already, they will have to fight for survival, too.

But in surprisingly large numbers, cities are fighting and winning. Old-school downtowns are coming alive. Small colleges are attracting students, and growing businesses are finding ways to attract talented people to build a life a little ways off the beaten track. The "American Urban Century" might look a lot different—and a lot better—if we're willing to see the change wherever it might be taking root.

My big takeaway from these road trips across Oklahoma, Texas, Kansas, and Arkansas is that the essence of what it takes to make a city great may not be easy to achieve, but it might be simpler than it looks.

To see what I mean, I invite you to a stretch of Highway 82 that crosses southwestern Arkansas.

A Tale of Three Cities

I don't have to check with the Census Bureau to know that southern Arkansas has serious issues with poverty and social decline. With about twenty minutes of research I could comb through the statistics and paint you a picture of desperation, poverty, and declining health. Most of the people that live here don't have the formal education you might find in other parts of the state like Little Rock or Bentonville. The people that live here have had to fight for themselves. This is no hot spot of innovation. No billion-dollar startups are likely to grow from this soil. But the people here are proud and patriotic, and there is a lot to learn and appreciate along this stretch of road.

Highway 82 is not exactly easy to find. Heading northeast from Dallas, you will learn that Interstate 30 takes a pretty hard turn at the state border in Texarkana. Interstate 30 was built to take you to Little Rock. If you want to continue east, across the southern stretches of Arkansas toward Mississippi, you will need to follow the signs that lead to Lewisville, Magnolia, and El Dorado.

The first thing you need to know about all of western Arkansas is that it is remarkably beautiful. The Ozark Mountains are gorgeous, and although the mountain ridges are located a few miles north of the highway, the view is still enjoyable. There is not much traffic, and other than an occasional logging truck, you will mostly have the road to yourself.

The railroad came here first. There is a Union Pacific line that appears to have created the trail and the towns you encounter along the way. The Red River crosses Highway 82 in a little town called Garland, reminding you that this part of the country gets more than its share of rain.

For me, the most interesting aspect of the drive along the highway are the county seats. Lewisville, the seat of Lafayette County, is first. County seats have a natural advantage over their rival small towns. First, they have government jobs. Working for the county in Lewisville has been and remains one of the best jobs in town. Second, county seats have their courthouses. The importance of having an old building like a courthouse should not be underestimated. A courthouse provides a town center. A courthouse can make an architectural statement.

If people in a community want to resurrect their town, they face a difficult challenge if they do not have a downtown. And even if there is a downtown, they really need to have some sort of town square or some specific focal point or community gathering place. Architecture is important. New investment will need something to build from.

If a town's gathering place is the local high school or one of its churches, it's going to be tough to attract visitors unless they are in town attending a sporting event or a church service. A community needs visitors! If you can't attract visitors, it's going to be tough to grow the economy. Visitors also restore hometown pride. People want to be proud of their community, and they want people to come visit.

For some reason, Lewisville has never grown very large. And it has never been very prosperous. Like most of these places, Lewisville grew in the 1950s and 1960s, but its population never reached more than about sixteen hundred. It is about eleven hundred today.

To review some key points: Lewisville is on Highway 82. It is a county seat. It has a county courthouse. It does not seem to have many visitors.

Let's keep heading down along Highway 82.

Just east of Lewisville, you encounter the small city of Magnolia. Things are different here. Like Lewisville, Magnolia is a county seat with a county courthouse. But the moment you enter town, you notice a difference. The citizens of Magnolia are working at, and succeeding in, building a community. The town square surrounding the courthouse is a delightful place with retail shops and restaurants. Southern Arkansas University is located here, so there's a regular flow of young people and a cultural energy that comes along with serving those students. Incomes are higher in Magnolia than in Lewisville, and the population here is increasing.

Let's stay on that point for a moment. The population is increasing. Very few rural cities of this size are growing. I don't want to mislead you. Magnolia is not growing much; in fact over the past few decades, the population has been pretty consistent at just over eleven thousand. But *something* good is happening here.

As you walk through downtown, you see amazing murals painted on the sides of buildings. Magnolia's leaders have obviously taken some risks and encouraged artists to liven things up. This is not as easy as you might think. Believe me, anytime someone comes up with an idea to paint murals on the sides of downtown buildings, someone else is going to say no. One man's art is another's vandalism, and there is no accounting for taste. But this city obviously embraces its young people and the art they can create. Magnolia is not afraid of change.

I can see why a visiting college student might choose to study here. If you come from a smaller town or a nearby city in rural Arkansas, Magnolia probably looks pretty happening. That's what urbanization is: People moving to places with more people than where they are from. People on farms are moving to towns. People in small towns are moving to bigger towns. Magnolia has figured out a way to attract people.

As a result of the quality of life in Magnolia, there are jobs there. Companies you would categorize as heavy industry are located here. Every May, there's the Magnolia Blossom Festival and World Championship Steak Cook-off. It attracts forty thousand people!

Here's something else to notice. The cook-off is a world championship *because the town of Magnolia says it's a world championship.* I am guessing a lot of communities would not have the confidence to announce that their local event is a world championship. The people that live in Magnolia are not afraid. They are obviously proud of their city—and they should be.

Okay, let's review: Magnolia is on Highway 82. It is a county seat. It has a county courthouse that functions as the architectural center of town. It has visitors. It has jobs.

Magnolia has used its assets. First of all, the name of the town is an asset. Saying the word "Magnolia" conjures up an image. They used the town's name to come up with the idea for an annual festival. They have a university. They have a courthouse. But the town's success goes beyond its historical assets. The leadership in this community took some artistic risks by encouraging murals on several downtown buildings. They organize and promote events. Even if a person grew up in Magnolia and moved away, I bet they come home for the holidays and stay a little longer, and talk about their hometown with pride. This is a cool place that is building memories and values life experiences.

I once heard an urban planner named Mitchell Silver say that previous generations were consumers of goods. New generations are consumers of experiences. His point was that when we build communities we should not be just designers and planners but experience builders. You can have experiences in Magnolia that are not inferior to those in big cities.

As we continue driving east on Highway 82, the road gets busier and the number of logging trucks begins to grow. Along the highway, the tall trees are beautiful, nearly creating a canopy over the road. This is a two-lane highway here, so it is best to not be in a hurry. Highway 82 is a road of places. And the best is yet to come. It is thirty-four miles east of Magnolia.

Welcome to El Dorado, Arkansas

El Dorado, Arkansas, is one of the finest small cities you have probably never heard of. It is, like the others, a county seat. This is the heart of Union County, located in south central Arkansas. About halfway between Hot Springs, Arkansas, and Shreveport, Louisiana, it is about an hour's drive of a town called Hope, where Bill Clinton was born, and an hour from Crossett, where Oklahoma coaching legend Barry Switzer was born.

Those are interesting tidbits, but in truth El Dorado is not really close to anything important. And it's not really on the way to anything important, either. But there is something important about El Dorado, and it offers us an incredible lesson.

Throughout the twentieth century, El Dorado was fortunate to have successful business leaders who were able to create good-paying jobs. The area was in the center of an oil boom in the 1920s. As you can tell by the number of trucks, the timber industry is very strong. But just because oil and timber companies thrived and supplied jobs for our grandfathers' generations doesn't explain why those industries are still thriving in El Dorado today.

You see, Oklahoma's ties to the oil industry are stronger than any in Arkansas. In the mid-twentieth century there were several Oklahoma-grown energy companies located in towns similar in size to El Dorado. But they went away. Some got bought by bigger companies; most went to Texas. The point is that it became virtually impossible for a growing energy company to remain in a town of twenty thousand people.

To grow, a company needs to attract new talent. They need to attract highly educated people. The city where the company is located has to have at a minimum an acceptable quality of life. That means it must offer a quality public education, nice restaurants, parks, sports, and a commitment to the arts. It needs elected leaders who are visionaries. It needs business leaders with high standards.

El Dorado, with fewer than twenty thousand people, pretty much has all of these things. They have a symphony orchestra, a performing arts center, two golf courses, and a private tennis club. They have a convention center. They have a daily newspaper and local radio stations. It sounds hard to believe, but El Dorado has two airports. And ten city parks. In 2011 they opened a new, $48 million high school. They have an impressive youth sports complex. It is not far from their arboretum and botanical gardens.

So how do they pay for it all? Like Oklahoma City, El Dorado passed a one-cent sales tax that they have used for infrastructure and quality-of-life improvements. It's a wonderful example of individual taxpayers and the private sector working with the public sector to encourage a higher quality of life for its citizens. El Dorado has invested in itself.

As you would guess, El Dorado is the home of several annual festivals that bring in tens of thousands of visitors. Downtown is built around a beautiful courthouse square and has fifty or sixty specialty shops and restaurants. In 2009, it was named a "Great American Main Street Award Winner" by the National Trust for Historic Preservation.

Some small towns still do well, sure. But wait, there's more.

Every graduate of El Dorado High School who was enrolled since at least the ninth grade gets a free college scholarship. There's a generous cap on the amount of the scholarship but it's good at any university in America. The scholarship is funded by Murphy Oil Corporation and championed by its CEO, Claiborne Deming.

"My wife, Elaine, loves to tell the story of her visit to a local jewelry store," Deming begins. "A big, burly guy that she didn't know approached her and said, 'I just want to hug you.' And with that he wrapped his arms around her and squeezed. He told her, 'My kids go to college, and they wouldn't have gone without you.'"

I noticed a long time ago that businesses with high standards don't stick around in cities with low standards. For that case, El Dorado, Arkansas, is Exhibit A. But this is just one example of dozens, even hundreds of communities like El

Dorado that have found new strength in being the right size at the right place at the right time.

What next-generation cities, from New York all the way down to El Dorado, all have in common, big and small places alike, are first a sense of community and togetherness that adds to the fundamentals: collective strength, quality of life, increasing population growth, and a plan for working together that feeds how people view their place in the world and think about the future.

A Thousand Engines of Innovation

Let me take a step back and guess what you're thinking. First of all, as nice as El Dorado might be, it is the exception not the rule. Most towns like that are suffering or emptying out, and with even bigger global economic changes than the interstate highway system coming their way, El Dorado might be up for the biggest fight of its life.

El Dorado also has something in Murphy Oil that only highly fortunate places share: a durable and loyal local industry that has seemingly no plans to move its headquarters and is willing and able to pump millions of dollars into the economy and downtown and keep jobs growing—perhaps even when it's not the best business decision. I mean, how many towns in America have a company willing, or even able, to put even ten kids a year through college, let alone every kid in the city? Smaller places have surprisingly big ideas, and as we think about the future of our country, it would be a bad idea to count them out just because of their size.

Maybe this idea of America in 2050 as a rich tapestry of diverse communities, of a hundred cities across the country as dynamic and "weird" as Austin, is a pretty picture, yet one that is impossible to achieve. Perhaps the country, really the whole world, is moving to cities, and it's foolish to try to reverse that tide.

In truth, however, I do believe there is something spectacular in the potential that still exists in towns of ten, fifteen, or twenty thousand residents. And with innovative ideas pouring out of many of them, we should take seriously the idea, and support it with our work and energy, that one of our country's biggest assets is the thousand places—whether El Dorado, Arkansas, or a single neighborhood on the outskirts of New York City—that have a lot to offer for our future.

In places like El Dorado, and several cities in my home state, such as Okmulgee, Weatherford, Miami, and a few others, we have places that have just enough size to think strategically about their economic future, and far more than enough of an entrepreneurial spirit to really get things done. Sure, the next Silicon Valley isn't likely to sprout up in their midst. But that's not what small towns were ever made for in the first place.

A couple things are pointing in favor of the El Dorados of the world. One is the surprising number of places that have a great employer like Murphy Oil. A recent *Washington Post* story—and many others like it along with my own experience on these road trips—tells the tale: The map is dotted with great small towns built on the backs of successful companies that are hiring like mad. The problem in these places isn't jobs. Not at all. The problem is attracting people to live there. It's not an easy sell, but a lot of places are trying. And if the trend of smaller cities punching above their weight continues, groups like the Strong Towns movement will have plenty of work to do.

The other is our country's unique ability to respond to what may be the biggest opportunity of the twenty-first century—the rising global middle class. Our twentieth-century prosperity was built on the rise of the middle class here in America and across a healing post-war Europe. Factories there were slow to rebuild—ours were in condition to feed those growing markets and manufacture the goods needed for growing cities. As the middle class continues to grow in Asia, Africa, and Latin America, the United States stands in a unique position to serve those growing twenty-first-century markets with innovative twenty-first-century products. In new manufacturing, digital economy, and development for the rise of smarter cities around the world, the United States can compete—and win.

Seizing these opportunities will be hard work. But I know the people in these small towns. And they know how to work hard. In fact, I'd be *surprised if we didn't* see dozens of places like El Dorado adding something crucial to the constellation of urban America in the decades to come.

Punching Above Our Weight

From 2009 to 2011, I made forty-five weekend trips to New York to earn an MBA at New York University. I can tell you that one of the great things about New York, and most of the other incredible "Superstar Cities," is that they often feel like a number of great, smaller cities sitting right next to each other. In your neighborhood, you have everything you need: your favorite dry cleaner, the best cheap coffee, and the best expensive coffee all within a minute or two walk. Each neighborhood has its own culture, schedule, geography, and genius.

The new development that I find so exciting is how lots and

lots of other islands away from the megacity mountaintops offer that experience at a better price.

If you happen to be a reader of Richard Florida and his work on the "Creative Class," you have an idea how the numbers show just how populous and prosperous the emerging, global Superstar Cities are becoming. It's impossible to argue that an elite class of incredible urban centers is rising in the United States and around the world. New York, Tokyo, London, Dubai, Shanghai, and a few other places form the commanding heights of the global economy.

But it doesn't take a huge leap to predict the downsides of overconcentrations of people, ideas, or capital. Already, we've seen blue-collar workers, immigrants and their families, college graduates, and many others making different choices, finding smaller places where they can build wealth and make their own mark on their cities.

From a more idealistic point of view, we should think about what new ideas and capabilities we can build if we support growth, creativity, and productivity in urban places of all sizes in America. To seize on our strengths, leverage our biggest assets, and respond to the opportunity of the rising global middle class, we need to build our own middles up, too. After the success of Dr. Florida's Creative Class in launching the current urban renaissance, perhaps we should be building a "Productive Class" to put our most creative ideas into action. And I know just where to start building.

CHARLESTON: WE KNEW YOU'D COME
IF YOU COULD

In a chandeliered ballroom at the U.S. Conference of Mayors in 1976, a first-year mayor of a small city, Mayor Joe Riley of Charleston, South Carolina, arrived at a committee meeting early and took the first seat he could find. Mayor Richard J. Daley of Chicago, who even fifteen years earlier likely had the power to swing the 1960 presidential election to John F. Kennedy, entered the room for the start of the meeting.

Daley noted young Mayor Riley sitting there, picked up his name placard on the table, and moved it to sit as an equal right next to his junior colleague. This may sound like a small nicety among mayors, but really it is an important thing to understand if you're sitting out there in a smaller town or a city with turnaround potential.

Know this: Your mayors are all rooting for each other, and all of us, a city's leaders included, want more than anything to crack the code of local development and build the momentum that can make every place great, large or small.

Many times, that leadership and sense of community comes from the top, but it also reaches all the way to people's daily lives and real-time problems. I have seen time and again how your mayors are openly rooting for each other and working together to make their city—and all the others—the best places they can be. This is really important to understand, and is one of the best tools we have to make our cities as great as I believe they can become.

As we think about the outsize power of smaller cities and midsize metros, it's important to take a deeper look at the work of one of the strongest mayors (and people) I've ever met. Once you read through this man's story, I think you'll understand a little more why even a titan like Mayor Daley would treat the mayor of Charleston not just as a colleague and contemporary, but as an equal. Because smaller cities, and mayors like Joe Riley, truly punch above their weight.

The only way I can think to sum up Joe Riley's place in the past and future of cities is to call him the "Mayor's Mayor." Joe served his city as mayor across five decades and forty years of the most tumultuous times in his city's and our country's history. Early in his career, he led on issues that feel increasingly prescient in our current political environment.

It is nearly impossible to pick a place in this book to write about all that Joe accomplished during his years of service. His leadership with developers and community leaders to rebuild the city's centuries-old, decaying downtown was among the first examples of its kind—his impact being felt in dozens of cities through the Mayors' Institute on City Design, which my teams from Oklahoma City credit with shaping our early plans for our own city's downtown reinvigoration.

His steady hand through the storm and aftermath of Hurricane Hugo, in 1989, was a precursor of the kinds of leadership we saw in Oklahoma City from Ron Norick after the bombing in 1995 and again from Mayor Rudy Giuliani in New York following the attacks of September 11, 2001.

What truly set Joe apart was the clear love he had for his city and the people he led as mayor, particularly how that love led him into his office and to the city's ability to heal deep wounds of racial division that had been ignored for decades. Not only that, but to turn that healing into a strength that would get them through unspeakable tragedies.

Charleston had been a city divided on racial and class lines—in the view of many, the wounds of the slave trade and the Civil War had never begun the process of healing. As a young man, Joe Riley was elected a member of the South Carolina House of Representatives, where he became a civil rights leader, not so much by accident, but rather by instinct. In only his second short address to the South Carolina House, Riley quietly and directly took the side of civil rights protesters in his city, among the all-white members of the elected body. All of twenty-six years old at the time, his fairness and compassion in the face of injustice caught the attention of African American and white leaders in the Charleston city council. Six years later the city had made him their mayor.

In his farewell address to the U.S. Conference of Mayors in Indianapolis in the summer of 2016, Mayor Riley took the stage to a crowded room, about a year after he had left office. He said his farewell after he had been gone so long, because in the days before that same conference the year before, the lives of nine parishioners at Emanuel African Methodist Episcopal Church were taken in downtown Charleston. When Mayor Riley returned a year later to that annual June meeting of mayors, the city of Orlando, and the whole country, was barely a week past the devastating attacks at the Pulse nightclub.

Mayor Riley shared with us a message about cities, and mayors, and what we can do for our people.

He told an incredible story about an elementary school presentation he had given years earlier, where a young man surprised the mayor and did not ask the question he normally got from elementary students—"How old ARE you?"—but rather announced with a heavy heart that his family had lost their dog the day before. The dog was found, and the mayor received a note from the teacher the next day saying the child was grateful for everything he had done. Of course, Joe hadn't needed to pay special attention to that case of a runaway family member, but the kid believed that the mayor and his team cared. And he was right.

And in what to me perfectly summed up his forty-year career and my relatively short four terms serving as mayor in my own city, he recounted a moment when a member of a family he knew suffered an unexplainable crime. Investigations were under way, but Joe made time in his schedule. When the city's mayor stopped by to pay a visit, the family said thank you and, "We knew you'd come if you could."

To be sure, that much is true of most presidents, senators, congressmen, and governors. They, too, would come if they could. With mayors, the difference is they can, and they do.

It is a special thing to be a mayor. Formally speaking, our powers are surprisingly limited. Our budgets are largely hemmed in by state and federal rules and regulations. Our policy-making authority is surprisingly narrow, especially given the broad range of issues our voters hold our feet to the fire to address. Some leaders might find this balance of ability and expectation unfitting or unfair. For most mayors, especially the great ones like Joe Riley, there's nothing we won't try to get done if we can.

Conclusion: The Path to Public Service

The stories of innovation and transformation in *The Next American City* come from different places, but they have much in common. One thing that surprised me looking back across the chapters: Though major accomplishments always take a team to complete, the seed of the idea is generally planted in the mind of one person. Christy Counts's vision for animal welfare in Oklahoma City. Mayor Greg Fischer's insight that individuals finding inner peace would help create a peaceful and prosperous city. Kevin Johnson's singular efforts to save a sports team he knew was critical, but never personally played for.

One person with a vision, the willingness to risk, and the openness to share their ideas with others is the place where big changes seem to always start.

About twenty years ago I caught a vision and made a change. I was definitely not formally trained for the responsibilities I was about to take on as I left journalism and entered public life. But I knew I was capable of more. If you feel the same way and have a desire to shape your city's future, or even change the world, I hope my story below helps motivate you to take the leap.

Decisions Happen in an Instant. Impact Takes a Generation

There have been many events throughout our city's history that changed its trajectory in an instant. The cannon fired into the sky that launched the Land Run of 1889 and built our city in a day. The afternoon of July 5, 1982, when Penn Square Bank collapsed, sending Oklahoma's economy (and perhaps the entire banking industry) into a tailspin. And of course, the morning of April 19, 1995.

Those turning-point moments, whether good or bad, seem to give us hints about the deeper changes afoot around us. If we are lucky, and we pay attention, we can use the turning points to better orient ourselves. That's how it was for me.

In the 1990s, when I was at the peak of my news career, the worst thing that ever happened to my city—the bombing of the Alfred P. Murrah Federal Building in April 1995—unearthed an unspoken sense of community, one that has made our city's transformation possible. It also changed my life.

Mick Cornett, Born Sportscaster

You frequently hear stories about young people who enter college with no idea of what they want to study. That was not me. From the time that I was ten years old, I had been preparing for a career in sports journalism. Those years of training led to something of a meteoric start in the business.

A few days after finishing my coursework at the University of Oklahoma at the age of twenty-one, I left Norman for a position as the main television sports anchor at the ABC affiliate in Bryan, Texas. Let's be honest: This was a huge job for a twenty-one-year-old to land. Not every moment was perfect in Bryan, but I learned enough to set me on the trajectory for a career I had always wanted.

Just a few months later, I was recruited to a much larger market in Eugene, Oregon. And just a few months after that, I was headed home. My third job promotion happened in the fifteen months since I had left school. I was to join the sports department at KOCO in Oklahoma City. I would work at my hometown ABC affiliate in a variety of roles for the next eighteen years.

Back in my hometown, I worked hard. I had enough energy, persistence, and knowledge of sports to compete and make a living in the highly competitive business of television news. And truthfully, this was nothing short of my dream job. Every day, I was watching sports, talking sports, writing about sports. And being paid pretty well to do it. Every year, I would travel to a bowl game or its equivalent and interview teams and coaches moments after they won the games of their lives. Every day brought a new challenge and new things to learn. I was doing well and having the time of my life.

But in my thirties, my interests began to expand. The change was subtle at first. For instance, I found myself choosing to read *Time* magazine instead of *Sports Illustrated*. This might not sound like a big deal to you, but remember, I was a guy who spent my spare time as a teenager memorizing sports statistics for fun. Who played in the 1925 World Series? Easy. Who played third base for the 1960 Pittsburgh Pirates? Even easier.

And now I was reading *Time*? Oh my God, what was going wrong?

Soon after that, I was reading books written by Tip O'Neill and Newt Gingrich. And I enjoyed them! At this point, I didn't know what I was becoming. Or, better said, what would be-come of me?

Sports are designed to be diversions. So when your life is based on a diversion, it creates all sorts of conflicting issues. When work is so much fun, your days off are not as exciting. What was I supposed to do on my day off, kick back and watch the game? That was a day at the office for me.

Starting to feel some frustration, I would spend my precious vacations wondering why I kept going back to my career on television. Could I run a corner store? Become a professional golfer? Start a business of my own?

After my trips were over, I would go back to the station and two hours later I was frantically working on the next deadline, forgetting all about my vacation daydreams.

Mick Cornett, Natural Comedian

Even though I seemed to be more interested in the serious side of life off-camera, my on-air persona was becoming more and more comedic. For my producers, this was no laughing matter.

In the 1980s, television was changing dramatically. Almost as fast as the Internet is changing today . . . Cable TV was giv-ing viewers more options than ever before. If you're under thirty it might be hard to imagine this, but for decades there were only three network TV stations to tune in to. Out of no-where, cable TV emerged and ESPN was beginning to build an audience of all-day sports viewers. Basically overnight, our news department needed to compete for our audience, and one way to do it was to entertain them.

And entertain them I did.

More and more, I became the sportscaster that made you laugh. Believe me, writing and performing comedy within the bounds of a nightly sportscast was not easy. But my managers at the television station couldn't get enough of it. It was something most other sportscasters could not do. Fans noticed and, like a preamble to today's hashtag, they would repeat my one-liners back to me on the street. Managers noticed, too, and so I was beginning to be paid pretty well to keep it up. It always feels good to be appreciated, and I felt it.

On the night of April 18, 1995, I was anchoring the ten o'clock news. I had worked something like twenty-five days in a row and was scheduled to begin a vacation the next day. Since it was my last night on the air for a couple of weeks, I decided to do something special.

Most local sportscasters are smart but not exactly Hemingway at the typewriter. Clichés like "he gave 110 percent," or "he ran like the wind," seem to be part of the shtick. Under a deadline, clichés become a crutch. I abhorred them.

I developed the discipline of never writing a cliché into my sportscast. Never. I took pride in the fact that I chose every word carefully and edited my copy with precision.

And then every once in a great while, like twice a year, I would write a sportscast with nothing but clichés. It was "Cliché Night." And it was a hit.

I would promote it. And people looked forward to it. I don't know that it is the type of humor that would stand the test of time, but it was good enough to keep the viewers tuned in. Calls and letters suggested the audience thought it was outrageously funny. Even today, almost twenty years later, people still stop me on the street wondering when the next Cliché Night might roll around.

That evening newscast of April 18, 1995, was no different. Cliché Night delivered the laughs. Duty complete, I was ready for a break from work. My family was looking forward to spending a couple of weeks on a regular schedule. I was anxious to clear my head.

When the Show Can't Go On

I got home about midnight, but it's not easy to get to sleep when you work so late in the evening. You are wound up. Around two o'clock, I finally fell asleep. After such a late night, I was still in bed and still groggy at nine the next morning when my house shook. It felt like some enormous burst of wind had passed through my neighborhood.

I was suddenly wide awake.

My wife opened the bedroom door and walked quickly toward the window that had a clear view of the front of our house. "I think a car just ran into our garage," she said as she opened the blinds to look. She was relieved to see nothing unusual.

I turned on the TV and then I watched as my television co-workers and our competitors at the other stations began to piece together the story of the largest act of domestic terrorism in United States history.

An extremely large bomb had just been detonated in downtown Oklahoma City. The concussion that rattled my house had traveled ten miles into the suburbs and still had enough energy to make my wife think a car had crashed into our garage.

It would be hours before we had a good sense of the details. Authorities were urging people to stay away from the scene. Within a day, media from all around the world were converging on our typically quiet city.

As you would imagine, everyone who was in Oklahoma City that day has a story. A life's journey that took a new direction. This is mine.

I spent the next several days at home while the television news media provided hour upon hour of local coverage. My bosses knew I was just starting a vacation. Just as well. No one had to say it, but in the midst of all this horrible news, there was no on-air role for the funny sportscaster. From a local journalism perspective, this was the story of our lifetime. My instinct was to be a part of it. But I knew better. I was useless.

So I was surprised when the station called and I was told my boss, Susan Kelly, was insisting that I come to work that Sunday evening.

Me? She wanted me to come in? What good was I at a time like this?

The city had never felt more depressed. By then, we knew more than a hundred people were dead and there were a bunch more presumably still buried in the rubble.

When I arrived, my boss said, "We are getting a lot of calls from viewers. Some of them are tired of the wall-to-wall coverage of the bombing. They want our newscasts to return to some level of normalcy." She paused as if she couldn't believe she was saying this. "They are specifically asking for you."

In all honesty, it sounded like some kind of joke.

Normalcy? You've got to be kidding! Was she delirious? After all, she had been working around the clock for days straight. I decided to put some sanity back into this conversation.

"We can't do sports at a time like this," I began. "I understand the human reaction of wanting to bury our dead and move on, but this is way too soon. We can't move on. Not yet. We haven't even found everyone yet!"

I was wrong about her not thinking clearly.

"Then tell them that," she said. "But you are going on tonight."

So I did it. I was on the air for about a minute. I talked to the audience in a calm voice and told them what I thought. I thanked the viewers who'd called in asking me to come on, and told them as truthfully as I could I just didn't think it was time to move on yet.

The reaction was overwhelming. I don't know the size of our audience that night, but it must have been bigger than normal. That one-minute speech would produce the only Emmy nomination of my twenty-year career.

That one-minute speech was also a turning point in my professional life. I didn't know it immediately, but the transformation that I had been experiencing for several years was finally complete. The funny sportscaster was gone for good.

For the next few months, I tried to figure out who I was. I fell into a comfortable on-air delivery style, which was more about information than it was about comedy. It worked. I was a professional and most of our viewers probably didn't even notice much of a change. But I noticed. And my boss noticed. She was trying to be patient, but I think she was a little concerned I was slipping into some level of depression. I knew I wasn't doing what I was meant to be doing. I didn't feel relevant anymore. Sports scores didn't seem important. So, the Cowboys beat the Giants. Who really cares? Certainly not me. Not anymore.

A Brief Flirtation with Public Office

By January 1996, I had been working a lot of hours during football season and, as a result, the station owed me some time off. I walked into my boss's office and told her I wanted to take a two-week leave of absence—I paused, because I couldn't believe what I was about to say—to look into running for Congress.

There was no expression on her face. She probably should

have fired me. A journalist, even a sports journalist, can't just take a leave of absence to "look into running for Congress." People would find out. It would reflect on the station. How would the station have any credibility if one of its main personalities had an obvious partisan slant?

She just stared at me. I think she was trying to figure out what to say. Finally, she broke the silence. "Okay." But that was all she said. It was more of a question than an agreement.

So I outlined my plan to her. I intended to talk to people inside the Republican Party and gauge my chances of unseating the two-term incumbent who was representing my district. In two weeks, I would return and let her know if I wanted to return to television or run for Congress. It all seemed perfectly logical to me at the time.

But after about five days of talking to people, several things became clear. For starters, I was *really* naïve. The Republican Party was thrilled I was interested in becoming a candidate for public office. But they offered no support in trying to run against an incumbent Republican. I hadn't realized that was the way it worked.

And then another really weird thing happened. The local Democratic Party found out that I was interested in running for Congress. They were anxious to meet with a "local celebrity" with an inclination to run for office. And, of course, they wanted to beat that two-time Republican incumbent.

I was such a political novice that I thought I should check it out. The next evening I wound up visiting with a woman who was an activist inside the Democratic Party. She sat me down and handed me a questionnaire about the political issues of the day. I filled it out and handed it back to her. She shook her head and said it wasn't going to work. Basically, I took a test on being a Democratic candidate and I flunked. Bad.

At least I was right about one thing: I was a Republican.

When I got back to the television station my boss, Susan, told me that she had not planned on my return. She figured I was gone for good. And maybe by this time she was hoping so. But back I came, thanking her profusely.

I was grateful she hadn't fired me, but I did end the conversation by giving her something to think about. "Maybe I should transition out of the sports department and become a news anchor," I suggested.

I was quickly becoming an expert in saying things she didn't want to hear.

But three months later she called me back into her office and asked me if I wanted to anchor the morning and noon newscasts for a week, just to try it out. This was exactly the news I needed.

A few days later she announced the move was permanent.

The Unique Allure of Local News

Perhaps I should have guessed it, but after you have anchored the sportscast for more than fifteen years, it's not easy to switch to news. It's a very different job.

Even so, I loved it. The work seemed relevant. It seemed important. There were stories about senior centers, and school closures, and a lot of stories about women's health. I had no idea what I was talking about, but I was trying to learn fast. I had loved doing sports for so long, but I had to face the fact that I was burnt out. As a news anchor, I loved going to work again.

The schedule was tough: up at one-fifty a.m., at my desk about three-thirty for a two-hour anchor shift at five, then I would do on-air updates inside *Good Morning America* and generally stay busy before anchoring a half hour at noon. I would go home in the afternoon, coach my kids' basketball teams after school, and get back in bed about seven p.m. You'd think it was a great life if you were trying to kill yourself. But the structure actually allowed me to live a healthier life, too. I wasn't in good physical shape, and I knew I could do better. So, I lost weight.

Once again, I was professionally motivated.

A year into this routine, management changed again and I had a new boss, Linda Levy. She was tough and she pushed us further than most of us wanted to be pushed. But knowing I could be more productive between my anchor shifts, I asked her if I could pick up a news reporting beat to cover between my morning and noon newscasts.

I went into Linda's office to convince her that I should cover the state legislature. After all, Oklahoma City is the state capital, and I still had an interest in politics. Sometimes I would daydream twenty-five or thirty years into the future. Maybe when I had retired from a, well, let's say a forty-five-year television news career, I might run for the state legislature. In any case, I wanted to learn more about what legislators did.

Evidently, my speeches needed some work. Linda listened and was glad I wanted an additional assignment. But she didn't want me covering the legislature.

"I want you to cover city hall," she said.

City hall? Why was she picking on me? What had I done to deserve this?

I didn't even know where city hall was. Literally.

But she was the boss, and I wasn't. So, I wandered over to the assignment desk and told the editor that I was his new city hall reporter. He hadn't seen that coming. But he was very positive about it. He didn't even laugh when I asked how to get there and where to park.

The city council meetings were held on Tuesday mornings with third-term mayor Ron Norick presiding. (At the time, Ron was highly respected but he was hardly the political legend that he is today.) I showed up at the meeting, picked up an agenda like I knew what I was doing, walked into the council chambers, and tried to fit in. Of course, I immediately failed at that. I sat off to the side, next to the wall, and watched as each council member noticed I was in the room, then did a double take. *Why is* he *in here?*

I figured they were stirring because they still thought of me as a sports guy, but there was more to it than that. You see, I didn't even know that the media didn't sit in the council chambers! There was a media observation deck on the next floor that overlooked the proceedings. With no idea what else to do, I instinctively started taking notes.

Sometimes you never know when your life is about to change. Given how crestfallen I was to get city hall instead of the statehouse, I obviously didn't see it coming.

But over the next hour? *I fell in love with city government.*

I loved the immediacy. I loved the idea of watching a citizen stand ten feet in front of their elected leaders and plead their case. I saw how personal and how emotional it could be.

When I got back to the station, I told one of my co-workers about my enlightenment and that city hall "is where the action is." The guy laughed out loud, thinking that I was trying to be funny. And then he *really* laughed when he realized I was serious.

Soon, my interest in city hall reporting was the talk of the newsroom. Everyone thought that I was crazy. They thought—and perhaps they were right—that anybody assigned to a city council meeting was being punished for something. But I was on the edge of my seat at every session.

I found an interesting story every week. There were some incredible personalities on the council, and all this conflict! Every meeting seemed to shed light on something that I had never considered. It seemed as though the stories that I told weren't being told by the other reporters. I think my advantage was that I didn't know what I was doing. And my new boss? She liked my work. And she wasn't an easy person to impress.

The following year, Mayor Norick retired and I covered the candidates in the 1998 mayoral race. I had no idea that the next time there would be an open seat for mayor, I would be on the ballot.

A year later, management changed again. The television ratings for my show were better than when I'd arrived but they weren't great. I knew that for what I was being paid, they could hire two younger people to fill my role. The crazy work schedule was wearing thin. My television career had run its course. Now what?

I knew I wanted to work for myself. I knew I wanted to make a difference. I knew I wanted a life of substance. That's about all I knew. And that was when my alma mater called with an idea.

Mick Cornett, College Professor

Let's back up a moment. About two years into that stint as a news anchor, a photographer walked by my desk and asked me whether I might be looking for a part-time job. I didn't exactly have spare time in my schedule, but I asked what it was anyway. Turned out my alma mater, the University of Oklahoma, was looking for an adjunct professor to teach broadcast writing. The photographer said I was the first person that came to mind.

This was a little ironic, because when I graduated from OU I remember thinking it was one of the best days of my life! I would never have to set foot in a classroom or write a term paper again!

But I had built a reputation among the station management as one of the best writers on the staff. In retrospect, I think they were wrong. Actually, I think what they saw on air was an ability to ad lib . . . and they just thought I was writing all that down in advance. But they told me I was a good writer so many times I started to believe it. I took the job at OU.

So, one night a week I got a bit less sleep than usual. It didn't pay much, but I enjoyed returning to my school to share ideas with a group of enthusiastic young people about to embark on careers similar to my own. Other than coaching youth basketball for my kids' teams, this was the first time I'd ever taught anything. I really enjoyed it—and little did I know the work would expand my whole view of what I was capable of.

When I left television, I decided to start my own business built around the skills that I had developed. I rented office space and bought a desk and two chairs.

The fact that I had two chairs showed some sense of optimism since I sat in one and there was nobody to sit in the other. Within a few months, I was starting to build a business that produced short films and corporate videos, and it was going okay. I was also building up a play-by-play broadcasting résumé, soon doing about fifty games a year. But the university called and offered me a full-time job as a visiting professor. Didn't see *that* coming! And I could still do the play-by-play and the video projects. And, this was important to understand, I worked for myself. It was fun. Not much financial security, but fun.

I taught the advanced television news classes and a few

writing courses. That was a fun year to be on campus. Bob Stoops had become the school's football coach and took the Sooners on an undefeated run through the football season. I was writing a weekly sports column for a local paper so I could still get credentialed to sit in the press box when I wanted.

So, I had like, what? Six jobs?

Emotionally, I was still hoping to find some sort of closure on all my years in television. The opportunity to teach was perfect. After twenty years of doing TV news, I was now able to step back and think about what I had learned.

What did it matter? Had I really made the world a better place? I had spent twenty years immersed in this endeavor and suddenly it seemed so meaningless. In the wake of the bombing, I wanted my life to mean something, and I couldn't see that the world was a better place for any of the twenty years I'd spent in television. I had worked on over twenty thousand broadcasts. Edited even more individual scripts and video clips.

Surely in all that work there was something memorable, something meaningful, something worthwhile? But maybe not. Maybe, in the grand scheme of life, it was just a waste of time. Which—wow, that's heavy stuff. You pour your heart and your soul into a profession and the world is no better for it. In the wake of the Oklahoma City bombing, and through the "meaning of life" struggles that followed, that was not a good place to be.

An Angel Disguised as a Delivery Man

And then one day, a really weird thing happened. I was working on a video project, and since I didn't own equipment, I was sitting in a small room at a production studio. I would hire a video editor to actually push the buttons to physically create the project. I would sit behind him in the editing booth and tell him what to do next. And since I was paying him $150 per hour, I was constantly pushing the process along. That hourly rate was like a day's salary for me, so once that clock started, I had no time for distractions.

The entrance to the editing room was open, and I heard someone knocking at the front door. I didn't work there, but I realized as the knocking continued that no one was around to see who had arrived. It was nearly five o'clock, and I had been so immersed in my video project that I hadn't noticed that everyone besides me and my editor had gone home. I really didn't want to break from my task, but opening the door seemed like the right thing to do.

It was a delivery man. He was fifteen years younger than me. African American. He had a dolly and a couple of small packages stacked on it. He was holding a clipboard, and I quickly summed up the situation. He needed me to sign for the packages he was delivering. All I wanted was to get back in that editing booth.

As he handed me the clipboard, he glanced up at my face for the first time.

"You're Mick Cornett!"

I had been out of television a year or two, but I still got recognized around town. I always tried to be gracious to anyone who seemed happy to meet me. So, I smiled and nodded.

"You're Mick Cornett!" he said again. But this time there was a different tone and inflection that I wasn't sure I had sensed before. Ever. And there were tears in his eyes. Now I was conflicted. I needed to get back in that editing booth, but he wasn't leaving right away.

"You don't understand," he said. "I watched you on

television every night. When you would come on, my dad would call all the kids in the house to come into the living room to watch. And when you were done, he would point at the TV and say, 'Now that's how you talk to people.'"

The tears were now on his cheeks. And there was a big smile on his face. "Never thought I'd meet Mick Cornett," he said as he repeated his father's line one more time. "Now that's how you talk to people."

And with that, he took back his clipboard and left. I didn't know what to say. I never got his name. Far as I know, I've never seen him again.

But somehow, in three minutes he had provided validation of a twenty-year career. I no longer had to wonder if any of my work had mattered. I could stop beating myself up for what I feared had been twenty years of superficiality. Twenty years of fluff.

And also, apparently, I had a skill I didn't know I had. Something to build the rest of my life around. *I knew how to talk to people.*

Mick Cornett, County Clerk?

In the summer of 2000, I had been out of TV for a year. A friend of mine named Mike McAuliffe was running a small advertising company, and he would hire me whenever a client needed a video project. So one time, we were in a tall office building in downtown OKC, where we had just finished making a pitch to a client. We were in the hallway waiting on the elevator when my cellphone rang. It was a political consultant who was trying to get me interested in running for a county office. It was a short call, but Mike overheard enough.

"What was that about?" he asked as we got on the elevator. I told him who it was and what they wanted.

"You could win that race," he assured me. "And it pays pretty well."

Most of my friends were kind of worried about my finances. I had about six jobs, and apparently that sends a message that you are struggling.

"I know. I could probably win it. But Mike, I don't want to be county clerk. What do I know about being a county clerk?" I kept talking. "You know what I would really like to do? I want to be on city council."

I had no idea that Mike had been at an afternoon meeting the week before with some passionate city hall supporters who were looking for new council candidates.

By the time the elevator door opened on the first floor, Mike was excited. I loved his enthusiasm but I thought Mike was missing one important variable. I lived in a ward with a popular two-term incumbent.

"They don't like him," he assured me, referring to the civic leaders who were candidate shopping. "He's one of the three they want to take out."

Mike introduced me to a group of leaders I guess we'd now call "urbanists," though Oklahoma City at that time was about the last place you'd expect to find a bunch of city and down-town enthusiasts. It was all new to me, anyway. It's embarrassing now to think of how little I knew about walkability, livability, historic preservation, and the basics of urban policy. The business leaders had to have known that about me, too. Even so, they were pretty sure I could probably beat that incumbent they opposed.

The Race, the Campaign, and My First Victory

These people I had never met adopted me as a candidate. They helped me raise some money and found a person to manage the campaign. I found out the mayor was supportive. I was grateful and flattered.

Meanwhile, I was working at OU as a full-time professor. So, as I was thinking through when to announce and how much money I needed to raise, I learned that you cannot work for the state and the city at the same time. The University of Oklahoma is a state institution. If I was going to serve on the council, I wouldn't be able to teach anymore. With the election in March and the transition happening in April, the end of the school semester in May wouldn't pose too much of a problem. I told the head of the journalism school that if I won the election, I would finish the semester but couldn't be paid, so I would just work for free. He was pleased with that but then told me he had changed his mind about my status as a temporary visiting professor. He wanted me to join the faculty for another year. It was too late. I was committed to running for city council, so I had to decline his offer.

My campaign manager could see I was all-in, so he got together a list of two thousand people who were most likely to vote in the next election. In a city as big as OKC, knocking on doors, especially in a city council election when maybe one in ten households makes it to the polls, is not a smart play. So I worked the phones hard.

Now, I don't know if anyone really expected this, but I called all two thousand of those people personally. Every last one. I admit I might have left a lot of voicemails, but I made the calls. My years on television were paying off. Most of the people who heard the message already felt like they knew me.

I also spoke to a few groups. My first speaking opportunity as a candidate was to the Oklahoma City Boat Club. I was scared to death. I realized talking to a camera was a completely different experience than talking to live people. Now I could actually see my audience. How weird was that? I remember someone asked me a question. I told them I had only been a politician for two days, and I didn't know the answer. They laughed with me.

My opponent did have a deep bench of donors, so a lot of the establishment politicians thought we were going to lose on election night. We didn't. We had a little watch party for the team at Buffalo Wild Wings, and our volunteers started bringing in the numbers from the different precincts. The polls closed around seven, and about seven-fifteen, the precincts tallied up the votes and posted the results on the door of the school or church or wherever the votes had been cast.

I picked up the results from one of those schools that served as a precinct, and the precinct captain recognized me. As he posted the final numbers, he said, "Young man, I think you're going to do pretty well." That was the first hard confirmation I had that I might actually be good at this. We won in a landslide. If I had lost, I assume I would have never run for anything again.

It was fun watching the news that night. My friends at the TV station got to announce my political victory. It was less than two years after I had sat on that very same stage. You could tell how happy they were for me. And three years later, I was elected mayor.

Daring the World to Tear Us Apart

My journey to the mayor's office started on the same day that dramatic changes came to the lives of my neighbors and friends. The Oklahoma City bombing took the lives of 168 people and changed the lives of thousands more. Including mine.

Looking back, I've come to understand that the changes that happened in my life and in our city started in a moment. In this case, a moment of tragedy.

What decided our fate is *how we reacted together*. We were suffering. We were at an emotional crossroads. And then, it was as if we, the citizens of Oklahoma City, reached down, pulled each other up, joined hands, and dared the world to pull us apart. The combined experiences of an economic collapse and a tragic bombing created a level of unity that otherwise could not have been achieved.

That unity led to this new golden age of civic pride and success. We went from having perhaps the worst economy in the country to potentially the best economy in the country in a span of twenty-five years. That may sound like a political eternity, but in truth it went by in the blink of an eye.

For years, civic leaders from all over the country have been coming to Oklahoma City to get a sense of the physical transformation of our downtown. They leave with more than measurements—they leave with big ideas. What they can't take with them is the sense of pride and unity that our difficult experiences gave us. It changed me; it changed all of us. To our great surprise, that change was for the better.

As I was sworn in as the mayor of Oklahoma City in March 2004, I was filled with ambition and good intentions. But I was also filled with doubt. This was the biggest assignment of my life.

At the time, I had never traveled overseas. Never met a former or sitting president. And I didn't know a single person who called themselves an urban planner.

I barely knew Mike Knopp and his passion for rowing. I didn't know Christy Counts at all. And David Stern was someone I might have asked for an autograph.

I was anxious to lead but I inwardly wondered if the city council and the city's leadership were willing to follow.

If you have read this much of this book, you are probably already in the game or standing on the sidelines wondering if you should run onto the field. Whatever you decide, work hard and have fun. There are doers and dreamers and we need both. Go make a difference.

The Next American City and the Future of the American Dream

As I read back through these pages, I realize it may sound a bit too optimistic. Perhaps all of this sounds a little idealistic to you. Or perhaps the idea that we could build in our country a network of as many as a hundred cities as impressive, globally connected, and fun to live in as Seattle, Austin, and Nashville is music to your ears.

You would be right to be worried. The kinds of markets, institutions, and economies that it would take to build a nation of a hundred Austins simply do not exist in this country, or anywhere in the world. And it is hard to imagine them coming into existence, especially in the toxic political environment that now surrounds us.

But isn't it our job as Americans to build things? To blaze

trails where no other country has gone before? Now that we've grown beyond the vision of a little house with a white picket fence, don't we need a new image that describes the American Dream? Maybe building the city of the future is the new vision we can all get behind.

The alternative, it seems to me, is admitting that the American Dream is on a long, permanent decline. Saying that, as a country, we had a good run there for a couple hundred years, but the challenges we face are just too much weight for our country to bear.

I don't know about you, but I refuse to accept that as our fate.

I think back again to the history books, and the pictures of great cities along rivers and against our nation's coasts. I think about what I learned in Oklahoma City, how we took that ditch that the grown-ups called a river and, with a bit of hard work, transformed what had been an eyesore into one of my hometown's true crown jewels.

I think back to the pioneering souls who built my city and populated our state—in that one day in 1889. I think of the Native American nations that came before us, whose ideals and values we struggle to live up to still today. And for a moment I remember the story of *The Grapes of Wrath,* about an era in our nation's history when those seeking opportunity, a better life for their children, or even just an honest day's work trudged across hundreds of miles of terrain, across the plains and over the Rocky Mountains.

Those were hard times, and our country found its footing not *despite* them, but *because of them.* What our ancestors did, and what we must aspire to do, is create the future we want to live in.

It is up to us to make things happen. To change; to compromise, of course; to place long-term social progress ahead of short-term political victories. To elevate country over our political parties, and then to rest assured that as we succeed we will create a better place for us and our hundred million new neighbors to call home.

So is the American Dream a thing of the past?

For the sake of argument, I ask you to think about the following:

Among the challenges we face as a country, which of them would have led the pioneers that settled our country to admit defeat? What policy issues or legislative debates would have led the Founding Fathers to admit that our Constitution and Bill of Rights had carried us as far as they could? What cultural, racial, and economic divides exist today that would have intimidated the thousands who fled religious or political persecution in other countries?

What about our schools and education? Do we not love our kids that much anymore? Infrastructure? Building bridges and highways too tall an order? Global competition? Other countries' workers too tough to beat? Or here at home, will we allow the fact that millions of talented workers and growing families still want to make their lives between our shores to be our downfall?

Have we lost our appetite to reinvent ourselves? Which hill, precisely, is too steep to climb?

As mayor, I would often speak to a roomful of twenty or thirty people. Enough to call it a crowd, but not so many I could avoid looking them in the eyes. I knew that in that room were Republicans, Democrats, Independents, Libertarians, members of the Green Party, and some people who didn't think about politics at all.

CONCLUSION: THE PATH TO PUBLIC SERVICE

But in moments like those all those people are in the room together for a reason. They are connected. They might be in the same line of business, have similar hobbies, or once have been high school classmates. They might live in the same neighborhood or their children attend the same schools. When it happens in Oklahoma City, I'm pretty certain they are at least all Thunder fans.

Our cities, states, and regions are bigger versions of these rooms. We're a very diverse nation, but we are all connected in real and important ways.

The similarities, however small, are important. It's time that we start spending more time concentrating on what brings us together instead of what tears us apart. As our population grows, I see an opportunity to reinvent and reinvest in ourselves by embracing our shared values.

In my office in city hall, I always kept a picture above my desk that I looked at every day. It's an old-fashioned photograph, and if you were in an antiques store it would just look like another turn-of-the-century shot of a dusty old downtown with a few folks running around a few ten-story buildings.

All of those things are true. But to understand the picture you have to know what would have appeared in the frame of that photo if it had been taken just twenty years before.

The answer?

Nothing.

At least nothing that looks like the city we live in today. The photo pictures downtown Oklahoma City scarcely two decades after the Land Run made that patch of dirt their new home. In the time it has taken our generation to wire most homes in our cities with access to the Internet, our ancestors built entire cities beneath their feet.

It might sound daunting to imagine that we could harness

the growing middles of American life into a dramatic transformation of our urban landscape. And I admit it won't be easy. But it is our country's legacy. And by historical standards, this is going to be business as usual.

The efforts are already under way.

Acknowledgments

I have many to thank and I must start in my own city. No mayor works alone, and certainly Oklahoma City's accomplishments have been the result of many people's work and achievements. Business leaders, working with city hall, have built a growing, diversified economy. Civic leaders like Larry Nichols, Clay Bennett, and Aubrey McClendon were far more important than any politician. Thank you. It's been an amazing journey for us all.

My immediate predecessors—Ron Norick and Kirk Humphreys—kept planting seeds that blossom today. Jim Couch worked for all three of us. Originally, he ran the water department. Later he took over the management of MAPS. He has been the city manager since 2000. If there's an overlooked constant in Oklahoma City's success, it is he.

Over fourteen years in the mayor's office, I have had three executive assistants. Fran Cory, Gayleen Keeton, and Karen Fox have, one at a time, kept me on time and in touch. There were also three individuals who served as chief of staff—Brett Hamm, David Holt, and Steve Hill. Each played important roles in my life and in our city's development. It was actually Steve who kept insisting that I write a book. And David? He is now the mayor. My goodness, how time has flown.

My middle-class parents insisted that I get a good education. That has opened doors I continue to walk through. If anyone questions the value of public schools, please call on me to respond. My teachers in the Putnam City school district were dedicated professionals. The University of Oklahoma created an opportunity for me to have a meaningful career in broadcast journalism. Hard to imagine I would have ever been the mayor without that career in television. And more recently, the professors at New York University helped me earn an MBA. Thank you to all.

In 2016, I was elected president of the United States Conference of Mayors. It's an amazing organization headed by Tom Cochran and Ed Somers. The knowledge and relationships I accumulated through the years with the USCM made this book possible.

In cities across America and around the world, I'd send a hearty thank-you to the hundreds of audiences who invited me to share our stories of reinvention. It is in your cities where I came to understand that while our story in Oklahoma was unique, we are far from alone in the work to rethink, rebuild, and restart the engines of prosperity across America.

Jayson White served as a wonderful coauthor of this book. I always have stories and ideas. I don't always know if they are interesting or good. Jayson has a knack for pulling together broad concepts and illustrating a more focused theme. He jumpstarted the project, unearthed the highlighted cases from dozens of incredible cities, and kept the project on task.

Working remotely, we spent hours discussing the work of other mayors and urban policy. He was a great teammate and added much to the finished product.

Jayson suggested we ask Mel Parker to represent us to publishers. That was a great decision. Thanks, Mel.

And of course the executives and editors at Putnam have been excellent. It has been fun, hard work with the best in the business, and I feel fortunate that they believed in us. Ivan Held, Mark Tavani, and Kerri Kolen have helped us understand the hardest lesson of writing: What doesn't fit in between the covers is often what makes a book great.

Providing essential background support: Neil and Kate Booth, Tracy Hilbert and Mercedes Robles, Michael Stransky, Jennifer Pollom, David Hochman, Will and Alethea Hein, Dave and Elizabeth Holmlund, Seth Hankemeier, Aaron Goldfarb, Ben Felder, and Jody Berger.

The stories across the chapters owe their existence to dozens of mayors, and several hundred interviewees Jayson and I spoke with over the years about this project. In no order whatsoever, I'd like to call out Jaana Remes, Jill Homan, Kristin Sharp, Jon Galante, Mayor Roy Buol, Aaron Renn, Vance Voss, David Parkhurst, Mitch Weiss, John Avlon, Mario Loyola, Marc Nager, Duriya Farooqui, Stephen Cheung, Morgan Day, Neil Kieiman, Julia Kraeger, Tim Williamson, Rob Lalka, Sarah Robertson, mayors Greg Nickels and Charles Royer of Seattle, Carolyn Zeilkow, Michael Lenox, Pete Furman, David Gogol, Skip Stitt, Jeff Kingsbury, and Mayor Stephen Goldsmith of Indianapolis, Mayor RJ Berry of Albuquerque, Ed Somers, Ed Redfern, Kenneth Quinn, Kunal Merchant, David Hochman, Ted Smith, Tony Peyton, Kerry Hayes, Stacy Richardson, Charles Wood, Kim White, Joda Thongnopnua, Frank

ACKNOWLEDGMENTS

Brock, Bratton Riley, and the inimitable Mayor Joe Riley of the great city of Charleston, South Carolina.

My family is always supportive and patient. I remind myself over and over again how lucky I am to have them. I am especially grateful for my wife, Terri. Thank you for sharing this journey.